AF227837

Brook Hollow Press

www.brookhollowpress.org

First Edition
978-1-7351252-8-2

HALF *a* WORLD AWAY

Nine Months Around the World in 1962-1963
Through the Eyes of a Young Boy

JONATHAN A. WRIGHT

"The fragrance always remains on the hand that gives the rose."
Mahatma Ghandi

Introduction

I am leaning over and peering down into a deep and narrow excavation hole near the harbor in Byblos, Lebanon, with my older brother next to me. Trucks are all around, honking horns, making deliveries to the boats tied up at the wharf, and picking up shipments, too. There are three men at the bottom with shovels, pencils, notebooks, and dusty canvas bags, handing small objects back and forth and talking in an unfamiliar language. They are excited and nodding their heads while taking notes and wrapping small items in old newspapers.

In layer upon layer, ten feet under the road, are the remains of seven civilizations, beginning with the Phoenicians and topped off with Crusader-era debris. All the recorded history here, in pot chards, iron fragments, and the brick rubble of everyday seaport life, is stacked up in distinct layers like a cake. It is early 1963, and barely a month earlier I had turned 11 years old.

My nine-month trip around the world took me to places that changed and shaped everything I have done, and dreamed of doing, throughout my life. The world's original hospice in rural France. Catacombs complete with loose bone remnants on their dirt shelves underneath sparkling Rome. The Taj Mahal awash in a full moon. The cave temples of Ajanta carved out along a sheer canyon wall. A mountain hike in shorts through wind and snow in Nikko, Japan. These were part of the timeless yet quickly changing world of 1962 and 1963.

These stories are autobiography, memoir, journalism, and history. My exposure to the broader world and witnessing of suffering across the globe provided a stark contrast with my family's own affluence. I was raised by historians, so the past, present, and future are always joined, contiguous, and often contagious. I saw a uniquely different world from atop an elephant in Cambodia, from the sampans of Bangkok, the Jeeps of the Himalayas, and from miles upon miles on foot.

I kept a journal entitled *Impressions, Ideas, Feelings,* and some portions have survived and are folded into this book. They became entry codes and passwords to a revelation of detail and story that continue to emerge. The rediscovered details are not imaginary. The entries are re-imaged from text and memory, with the flashlight of a postcard or photo shining into a forgotten place and bringing it forward.

The stories are written in my voice of that time, in the language that I knew at that age. Sometimes, recollections have melted like hot wax or been dusted over like donkey tracks in an arid land. Then, with a change of wind or light, I can look at a picture, smell boxwood, see a mountain range line, and images will begin to return, to move, and to solidify.

Over the course of those nine months, my writing became more practiced, my observations clearer, and my understanding of my family's privilege came more sharply into focus. Making this book has taught me how to drop into a scene or moment and see it afresh. I can taste and smell what was being served for dinner; I see the lighting and décor. I can see me there, trying to avoid the stares of the beggars and the holy men.

Like the view down through time in the Byblos excavation, these recreated events are loosened and processed from my deep back-mind, now seen again in my 70s. The entries begin in September 1962. Some are taken from daily writing assignments during our family's stay in London and other cities. Several early entries look back to the summer leading up to our departure from North America.

My parents assigned and entrusted to me the family Balda 35 mm camera, allowing me to load and unload the film unsupervised. One long roll of 36 Kodak Plus-X, chronicling our travels from Amsterdam to Venice, did not engage the winding sprockets, so the only visuals are those emblazoned in my memory. I am grateful for my family collection of postcards that we bought along the way, nearly 1,000 of which have survived, tucked away in my closet for half a century.

My fellow travelers were my parents, Mary and Arthur, my brother Duncan, 20 months older than I, and our tutor, Christopher Lydon, who had just graduated from Yale, where our parents taught. He folded into and around our family graciously and lovingly. It was the dawn of long-distance jet travel.

We were assigned correspondence-school teachers at the Calvert School in Baltimore, Maryland. During our longer stays in London, Paris, and Tokyo, we churned through double Calvert lessons each morning and then adventured with Chris, and sometimes our parents, in the afternoons.

We stayed two months in London, one month in Paris, and then, at the end of the trip, two- and-a-half months in Tokyo. In between, our itinerary took us through Italy, Greece, the Middle East, India, Southeast Asia, Hong Kong, and Taiwan. The longer stays were designed to optimize our parents' scholarly research and provided the framework for focusing our traveling "schoolhouse." Chris, resilient and funny, expected us to write a theme, or essay, several times each week. And so, we did.

Chris came from Boston and attended Roxbury Latin School. He had been an intern reporter at *The Boston Globe*, long before any of us knew he would become an acclaimed newswriter, television anchor, musician, one-time candidate for mayor of Boston, and a beloved radio host. During this trip, Chris was the very first writing teacher for both Duncan and me.

Later, Chris, aka "Chrissy Boo," would introduce me to Meg Kelsey, the love of my life, at the converted carriage barn on Chestnut Street in Boston where the Lydons made their home. We keep in touch still, even while his demanding journalism career has taken him to hosting Radio Open Source on WBUR in Boston.

How on earth did this come to pass? In 1959, my parents had secured the first married-couple-adjacent-tenured appointments at a major university. Their relocation agreement included year-long sabbaticals after just three years of teaching. The trip came at a unique time in world history, and in the history of our family. Our paternal grandfather died in 1958, so there were additional funds available to Arthur as an only child. We were highly privileged.

The trip had many elements of a grand journey with very comfortable accommodations. I saw the majesty of great architecture and stunning history alongside the poverty, the subjugation, and the suffering of ordinary people.

Our parents were alive and all aglow, yet during this trip there were also shadows darkening, presaging a time of emotional turmoil and illness, as well as substance use. The burdens of brilliance, knowledge, and life at the forefront of many things were heavy. Just seven years hence, Mary would die of cancer, and then Arthur six years later.

Arthur was an Oregon native, the first in his family to attend college. Stanford was the expected and unquestioned destination for promising young Westerners. At age 14, he had already traveled on a Pacific-circling cruise aboard the S.S. Malolo for seven months during 1928 and 1929. Asia captured him and never let go. He studied at Oxford with Arthur Waley, then at the Sorbonne, and arrived at Harvard in September 1938.

Mary was an Alabama native, the eldest of four daughters, who set out on a trip to Asia as a young teen, courtesy of her great uncle, Congressman William "Buck" Oliver. Her mother was the first woman to matriculate at the University of Alabama where she studied all things with passion and intellect.

Mary also arrived at Harvard in the fall of 1938, fresh from Vassar, expecting to study European history. But conversations with Professor John K. Fairbank changed all that, and her passion became modern China. She learned the language and history quickly and began on a path to become a world-renowned expert on modern and revolutionary China, as well as southeast Asia.

Our parents met in the Fairbanks' living room in the fall of 1938, and they married in the summer of 1940. They set out that autumn for the Far East, as it was called then, landing first in Japan and then in China, where World War II would soon find, detain, and engulf them. They were interned in the Japanese camp at Weishen until late 1945. That is another story, one that made them yearn to return to China.

Within the safety and privilege of this unique trip, my perspective on the world changed. The world shrunk to my scale and came in close. So many of the world's people were suddenly closer together, more familiar to me, and gathered on a single planet. I saw many forms of worship, and many of the great monuments amid urban chaos had a grandeur totally unfamiliar to me. The protections of childhood fell away. What was known and comfortable to me cracked open in rural India and in the mountain towns of Nepal.

When we returned home nine months later to six years of boys' private schooling, I was the youngest, and most widely traveled. I could not express it then, but I brought home a nascent passion for justice and for change in the world order, reinforced by the unfolding horrors of the Vietnam War. I did not much like some of the forced regimes of schooling during those years, sometimes excelling and sometimes resisting mightily.

I was sensitized from my wide array of experiences and I had things to say. Poetry and creative writing offered a welcome shift from the clumsy burdens of schooling and a shift into another realm, also half a world away from the routines of schooling.

The trip fueled my lifelong interests in architecture, design, building, spiritual practices, and wide-ranging cuisines. Watching brass being turned in Kathmandu or sandalwood carvings being made by hand piqued my interest.

The entry in this book featuring hotel architecture in Bombay, unlikely as it may seem, is nearly verbatim from my journals. Many more entries are based on stories I have told in part over the years. Here, for the first time, I have written them down and unfolded their many layers and textures. The daily details of the itinerary are partially as-recorded and partially deduced as to particular events on certain days, such as the opening of Parliament in 1962, or the dates of the London Auto Show.

Boy, it sure is a mixed up building. I get so confused with Victorian Bay Windows, Indian Balconies, a center dome like that on St Pauls in London, and corner domes like those of an Oriental mosque.

Bombay journal entry from January 1963

Appended to the journal entries in the red spiral-bound note-book are pages that list every plane flight taken including the airline, aircraft designation, engine type, and year of manufacture. I was keenly interested in all aspects of navigation, stars, machinery, and flight.

Once in a while during the writing of this book, I needed a refresh or a prompt. A link. For example, I could not remember the destination of our Bombay Harbor ferry ride, although I knew it involved an island. My memory of that morning was as hazy as its weather. But a quick internet search brought me to Elephanta, and within moments, the harbor mist and haze cleared in my mind. I remembered the ferry docking and walking down the two-plank-wide gangway, with its sagging rope handrail on one side. I remembered the smell of the eucalyptus, the path to the temple, and the faint ocher and green paint residues on the stone walls. These apertures into the past, once opened, have stayed ajar.

My brother Duncan has an adjacent but not identical set of memories. We sometimes joke about being raised in different families! Yet, when I mentioned my visual memory of a few days in Amsterdam, and the smell of hot chocolate at breakfast overlooking the canal, he quickly said, "Oh, yes, the Hotel Krasnapolsky." I recognized the name aurally right away and then confirmed that the hotel lobby and dining rooms offered views of both a canal and the Dam (the Dutch word for a dyke but also used to identify the main square in cities). The hotel name and other supporting details here are courtesy of Duncan, which I gratefully acknowledge. The trip (and my entire childhood and adulthood) would have been a lonely and desolate place without him. And I would have had to be the eldest child, which I would not wish on anyone.

The time of our travels was a narrow window, after Eisenhower's presidency and before the Vietnam War, enlightened by the broad hopes for America and all the world ignited in part by the election of President John F. Kennedy. The time after we returned would be defined for Americans in new ways, following the assassinations of John F. Kennedy, Rev. Dr. Martin Luther King, Jr., Malcolm X, and Robert F. Kennedy.

But during our trip, we were safe, the currency was good, and ethnic and regional extremism was nascent but not overly volatile. It was a late, perhaps the last, chapter in the European imperial and colonial age, and many stories reflect that unique period. The Middle East still showed the partition lines of European claims going back to the Middle Ages.

While we ate safe and delicious food and slept in clean, comfortable beds with private bathrooms, the trip showed me the suffering, injustice, longings, and poverty of children my age around the world. These made a deep impression on me, reaffirming my mother's unspoken passion and challenge to learn, to thrive, and to create, in hopes of changing the world for the better.

The trip also revealed our parents' preferences and passions. Arthur, in particular, would often comment on the status of Chinese institutions and culture, so advanced at almost any historical period when compared with the rest of the world. He reveled in ancient design and artistry. Mary was revealed as a keen and vigilant observer with a remarkable level of fascination and enthusiasm.

Throughout the book, I have used nomenclature and place names typical of the era of the trip. Thus, Bombay, Benares, Moslem, and other now-outdated names appear that have since been replaced with better Romanization, closer phonetic accuracy or a stripping away of colonial misunderstanding.

I mean these stories to provide refreshment, challenge, and wonder for all readers, as they have for me, whatever your experiences. Along the way, they also provide documentary evidence of a lost time. I have been inspired to tell the stories as fully as I can, so they may furnish encouragement to others to tell the stories that matter most to their family and communities.

ITINERARY

1962- 1963

1. LONDON

2. AMSTERDAM

3. PARIS

4. VENICE

5. ROME

6. ATHENS & NAFPLION

7. ISTANBUL

8. BEIRUT

9. BOMBAY & AURANGABAD

10. NEW DELHI & AGRA

11. BENARES

12. KATHMANDU

13. CALCUTTA

14. RANGOON

15. BANGKOK

16. PHNOM PENH

17. SIEM REAP

18. HONG KONG

19. TAIPEI

20. TOKYO, NIKKO, & KYOTO

To Hawaii

England

Tower Bridge with Thames tour boat

September 24 – A Palace on the Thames

THIS PAST WEEKEND, our very first in London, was fine and sunny weather, so our parents organized a Saturday family outing for all five of us to Hampton Court. The day felt a lot like late summer or early fall at home.

We took a water taxi up the Thames River, which flows right through the middle of London and down to the ocean. There were about 20 people on the boat, all out for a weekend trip. We passed docks with barges, small row boats, bigger river boats, and some boats that seemed to have been forgotten and were rotting away. Here and there a sailboat mast poked up along the crowded riverside. Some older boys were rowing long, skinny boats with four people rowing and one boy yelling from the stern.

Hampton Court was the closest country palace of King Henry VIII, and all his six wives lived there at one time or another. He had one of them killed for treason, and he had others killed, too. After the trip, Chris had us read up some more from the guidebooks about the history so we could figure out more of what had actually happened. I always have lots of questions, and Duncan does, too. I usually believe the stories, but Duncan is sometimes not so sure.

Anyway, Hampton Court really was a big and very grand place, with beautiful brickwork and stonework, and perfectly kept-up gardens everywhere. The grass had not a single weed in it. I had never seen bushes clipped and shaped to look like animals and birds, and I watched a man trimming the wings of a large bird, but it was really a plant. We were told that it took many years to shape a bush into a bird or a fox or a bear.

Inside, the floors and woodwork were full of many different beautiful woods and patterns. The furniture and paintings went on and on, with more than 30 apartments just for the King's guests.

A famous architect from London also designed many buildings at Hampton Court in the years after King Henry's time as a king. But then all the royalty ran out of money for their fancy things and Queen Victoria made Hampton Court into a museum and park.

When we got back to the train station in London, it was crowded with people trying to move on and off the platforms. We were working our way through the crowds, and I held Chris's hand and Duncan held Mary's.

Suddenly, there was a loud gasp from everyone in the platform area, and the crowd just fell away. Two policemen were running by, chasing a thief. Very soon afterwards, the police came back holding the guy with his arm behind his back. No handcuffs that I saw. One of the policemen, who are called Bobbies here, was carrying a green woman's purse, the one that had been stolen. Those guys ran fast and had no guns. Just a varnished wooden stick like a sailboat tiller, if they needed it.

The owner of the purse, all dressed for Saturday visiting, with a hat and veil even, was very thankful, I think, and she walked back with the Bobbies to make a report, Arthur said.

September 26 – Outfitting in Manhattan

Downtown Manhattan shopping, summer 1962

CHRIS ASKED US TO WRITE A THEME, which was a school-word for a story, on any topic we wanted. He did this almost every day. I had not told him about what we did during our summer before we met him, especially the trips to New York to get ready for the start of the trip. So, this story started as one of those themes.

In July, on a really hot day, we all got into the Chevy station wagon right after breakfast and drove to the New Haven Railroad Station to take the train to New York. We went there to go shopping at Abercrombie and Fitch and other stores, where they sold lots of things people needed for traveling.

The train had cars up at the front with faded dark-red velvet seats, in what they called parlor cars. We sat there swiveling back and forth, had snacks, and used the bathroom which flushed out onto the tracks. I held the hopper handle open for extra time just to watch the wooden timbers go by and listen to the clickety-clack of the iron wheels. On the left side of the train were the harbors and rivers feeding into Long Island Sound. Lots of boats were on their moorings facing north, which meant the tide was going out of the rivers. Boats anchored farther out, in the open Sound, faced west, also into the outgoing tide. Duncan and I are sailors so we always want to know where the tide and wind are coming from or where they are going.

We took a taxi from the station uptown to Abercrombie and Fitch, which is in the middle of the city. We walked into the store and up to the second floor on the escalator. There were lots of old suitcases in our attic at home, but Arthur explained that traveling by airplane meant we needed very light suitcases because the airlines weigh everything. Our parents looked at blue ones and brown ones. They selected the brown ones, which were heavy canvas wrapped over a tubed metal frame and so were really light.

Our parents each bought a large suitcase with a zippered top. Duncan and I shared a smaller bag of the same kind. They also bought a "carry all," a soft zippered bag for all sorts of loose stuff other than regular clothes. And finally, the "shoe bag," which was set up with cloth dividers into compartments like a wine box. Each compartment held one or two pairs of shoes, and our parents packed all kinds of other things in there, too, especially cigarettes and medicines, along with bottles and bottles of Arthur's special hair stuff called Pro-Ker.

It was time for a late lunch after Arthur paid for the suitcases through a tube going up to the store offices. Everything they bought would be delivered by Railway Express to the New Haven station. They found a small shop on a side street, and the roast beef sandwiches with mustard and a pickle were very good. Mary had tunafish salad with lettuce and tomato on toast, and she said it was very good, also.

We then stopped at a store called Saks Fifth Avenue and we bought shoes and clothes. Duncan and I got crepe-soled leather Oxfords that I was now wearing every day, and leather-soled dress shoes that were made by Bally in Switzerland. Those were for dinner out and special occasions. We got long pants, shorts, knee socks, V-neck sweaters, and blue blazers. Our parents bought all kinds of things for themselves, too. Arthur liked almost anything that was English and so wore shorts and knee socks when it was warm and the occasion more informal. All these items were sent to our home, so we did not have to carry everything to the station and then onto the train.

The train ride home was about the same as the ride in, except there was a dining car where Arthur bought Cokes for Duncan and me, and cold beer for Mary and himself. This was not usual, but they said they were relaxing.

Summer was ending and as the time to leave for our trip came closer, my friends at home were going back to school at Calvin Leete Elementary School in Guilford, Connecticut. The school was calling Mary wondering where we were. It's a law that we were supposed to be in school, and where, exactly, were we? They wanted to know. We were at home, but not for long!

September 28 – Needles and More Needles

For more than two months last summer, we all had two shots almost every week as part of getting ready for our trip and the many different diseases we might find. Every Tuesday and Friday, we went to Dr. Merman's office in Guilford to get shots for cholera, hepatitis, smallpox, diphtheria, encephalitis, and more.

The worst ones were the typhoid and the typhus shots—my arm swelled up and I felt sick to my stomach for two days after each of those. Mary explained that the shots contained a little bit of the disease, just enough to get us to build up resistance for our visits to foreign countries.

Just about the time I started to feel better, it was time for another shot. Sometimes we got two on the same visit, one in each arm.

One Friday in August, we had to drive into the Battery in New York City, which was way down at the south end of the city. This was where immigrants came in from other countries, stopping first at Ellis Island. We saw the island off to the right out in the harbor, but there were no ships tied up there on that day. The ferry to visit the Statue of Liberty also leaves from the Battery, along with other ferries to Staten Island, which was off in the mist.

The Battery got its name from the forts that were there, built to protect the city from the English and from pirates.

We had driven down to the Battery on the West Side Highway

next to the Hudson River where many ships were tied up at the piers. It was hot and dusty when we got there, and we lined up for our yellow fever shots. It was the only place you could get them, and they had to be kept cold. Then back in the car and three hours to get home—I felt so sick.

Once we were in London, all that seemed very far away. It sure seemed like a long time since we had left home, but it had only been a few weeks. I wondered what my friends, Ralph Tower, who lived down on Great Harbor, and Willy Shain, who lived over on Mulberry Point, were doing. I never really said goodbye or anything.

October 1 – Leaving Home

New TWA terminal, Idlewild Airport, 1962

THE LOCAL TRAVEL AGENT who planned the trip for our family had spent many months using telegrams and lots of telephone calls to New York to plan out the hotels, tickets, and preparations. He seemed a little nervous about remembering all the details.

Our parents were like that, too, with so much to think about. But everyone was excited, too. Mary called this being "keyed up." The agent had offered to drive us to the airport in our Chevy Parkwood station wagon.

Once the car was fully loaded with the luggage, we had a last lunch at home of sandwiches from the Guilford Deli on the green, and then we piled in. The two men were in the front, and I was in the middle of the back seat on the hump between Mary and Duncan. The wayback was fully packed!

Once we got onto the Connecticut Turnpike, the agent said he was not used to driving such a big car and mentioned it was hard to control the swaying and "tail-wag" of the back of the fully loaded wagon. Arthur reassured him, but that didn't help me, as my stomach was getting upset from the slow swaying motion. And it kept getting worse.

Mary noticed that I was pale and sweaty, so she let me put my head on her shoulder and then I fell asleep. I did wake up several times when we drove through the tolls where they have those baskets to throw in quarters. The travel agent missed one time and got out to try to find the coin, but it must have gone in the drain. Must have been quite a piggy bank down there!

As we got into the airport area, there was lots of traffic with trucks everywhere. Hundreds of planes leave every day, and the meals have to be cooked at the airport for most of those flights, so there were lots of trucks with meat, bread, and vegetables!

Arthur pointed out a brand-new building just being built that was completely different from all the others, which were all basically boxes. The new building was a whole separate terminal just for Trans World Airways and was designed by a very famous architect from Finland. Too bad we were not planning to go to Finland on this trip! Mary said it was a long way farther north from our planned route.

The building looked like layers of horseshoe crab shells overlapping each other with glass under the long curves. Arthur told us the building was all concrete and I thought it had a feeling of birds and wings.

Arthur was a big fan of flying. Why would we spend six days on the ocean when we could spend one night in an airplane six miles up in the sky and then be in London right after breakfast?

Anyway, once we got to the airport, we were helped by a porter in a blue uniform with red trim who was very nice to Duncan and me. Overhead we could hear the propeller planes taking off, and also some jets, which were very loud. It was really noisy inside too, with all the announcements and people talking, trying to be heard. People were leaning forward over the airline counters to hear. Each bag was being weighed separately, and I watched the big needle swing up for each one.

An Air France plane was getting loaded for a trip to Paris, and so was a United Airlines flight to San Francisco. The airport signs were in English and also two other languages, which Mary said were French and German.

It was partly cloudy outside, but no big storms were coming, I was told. I kept asking for some ginger ale to help my upset stomach. Finally, Arthur found us a place to sit down, and I had a Coke instead, which helped a lot.

October 3 – Just Stars and a Compass

WE HAD BEEN LOOKING FORWARD to seeing our tutor Chris Lydon again at Idyllwild Airport in New York. He had come out to visit our family at home in the summer, and we liked him right away— we were really excited that he would be coming with us. Actually, Duncan and I wanted a salty sailor from Maine who was a student of Arthur's to travel with us, but our parents always had their reasons. We were very happy to be with Chris.

It had been a busy end of summer for everyone except Duncan and me because we did NOT start school with our friends. We had put the boats away for the winter and covered them up with tarps laced down tight against snow and ice, but then we were pretty much done. Our feet were tough from running barefoot all summer on the gravel and sand, but after a few days in shoes, that skin kind of just falls off.

Arthur had all five sets of airline tickets, which included all our flight reservations for nine months, bundled with rubber bands in his leather briefcase. It had a flip-up lid with file folders in it and with his initials stamped in gold on the outside. In those lid pockets he also kept money, passports, and other documents. They were stuffed and kept closed by adjustable buckles and straps.

Each set of tickets was about four inches thick with carbon copies to tear off at each airport, and there were three sets per person, I think. He had letters addressed to banks in order to get money and a thick envelope of all our records of shots. I had asked him about his briefcase because I wanted to know.

Anyway, that first night out of Idyllwild Airport was aboard British Overseas Airways Corporation Boeing 707. Stewards on the BOAC flagship airliner served a British dinner from a silver trolley—roast beef, roasted potatoes, and peas—on china plates. I think Mary had Dover sole. We each had a silver knife, fork, and spoon, with white linen napkins, too. Arthur said they were copying what was done on ocean liners.

The airplane had four Rolls Royce jet engines, reclining seats, and a large smoking section that spread cigar smoke everywhere after dinner. Up in front, the pilots' cockpit door was kept open. The stewards served rich black Indian tea with plenty of sugar cubes and creamy milk. For the grown-ups there were small drink bottles with ice, olives, and other ingredients. Our parents were glad to have their martinis once we got into the air.

The pilots flew as fast as the plane could go—more than 600 miles per hour according to the pilot on the speaker. I read the BOAC magazine in the seat back pocket to get more details. In addition to the 707, BOAC flew the Comet 4 Jet, which had engines built right into the wings where they join the cabin, instead of hanging down off the wings. It looked really sleek. They also flew four-engine Britannia propeller planes for some of their routes all over the world, including to India, Australia, Hong Kong, and South Africa, according to the brochure. We flew to Antigua last year on a Brittania plane.

Duncan and I each had our blue-green BOAC cabin bags for Kleenex, a story book to read, a toothbrush with a small tube of

Ipana toothpaste, and a pad of paper with pens and pencils. Mary had something she called a reticule, which was really just a huge purse with a snap flap at the top. Everything was in there, from band-aids to airplane slippers! Mary also always carried our family's tiny little Olivetti typewriter under her seat.

It was hard to sleep because I was excited. Duncan dozed a little and I probably did, too. Chris was reading and then sleeping. I kept leaning out into the aisle and looking forward to the front of the plane. I could see the glow of green and red lights on the instrument panels through the open cockpit door, and the darkness of space beyond.

Only a few airlines made the trip across the Atlantic each night, I was told, and some only twice a week. So, maybe ten planes were out over the whole ocean tonight.

The clear night sky overhead gave the pilots stars to use for navigation. Just that and a compass was all they had. They pointed out the glow of Boston below on the left, and then a few tiny lights of Nova Scotia and then Newfoundland also off the left side of the plane, before we went out over the North Atlantic. We were going to fly over Greenland and near Iceland.

As the light of dawn began to show, breakfast smells filled the cabin. Scrambled eggs, bacon, and racks of warm buttered toast, with pots of strawberry jam and chunky English marmalade appeared on the silver trolleys, along with a separate cart of coffee, tea, and sweating silver pitchers of ice water.

Soon the pilots told us to watch for the lights of Ireland, and then for lights on the coast of Wales!

The pilots could get radio signals off the coast of Ireland as we got closer, to bring us in over Dublin, Ireland, then in toward southern England. Flying was a little like sailing but really fast. It was cloudy but the beacons directed the pilots down to London airport. They landed on the wet pavement at about 220 miles per hour.

As we drove into the city in the early morning, London was wrapped in misty clouds, fog, and smoke from burning coal. The smells got stronger as we got closer to the city. Two black Austin diesel cabs carried us to the hotel, one for us and a separate cab coming along behind with the luggage. Arthur rode in front, and Chris and Mary rode in the back seats. Duncan and I had folding seats called jump seats.

Arthur paid the drivers with different money, called Pounds Sterling. They have pennies called pence, and all sorts of other coins such as Crowns and Shillings. He had exchanged money at the airport while we waited for the luggage.

I started to realize that I would not be home again for almost a year, with so many new places in between. I really wanted to see the room where Duncan and I would be sleeping for the next two months.

October 4 – Our English Breakfast

ALL FIVE OF US SAT DOWN FOR BREAKFAST together in our suite of rooms on the fourth floor of the Old St. James House, as we did every day once we got to London. Chris had his own hotel room on the second floor in the back.

Old Saint James House, London

Duncan and Jonny enjoy their full English breakfast

I knew it was a cold and wet day outside because I could feel a little wind coming in around one of the windows. The main heat was from a Shilling heater in the fireplace. I don't know what was inside it, but you could put a coin in, and heat came out for a while. The ticking sound and the warmth blowing out was really nice.

Breakfast was brought to us on a rolling trolley by the same waiter as usual, whose name was, I think, Tommy. The elevator was run by a very small man named Brian. He sat in the corner on a built-in folding stool near where he had a rope, and he seemed to pull us up and let us down each trip. He wore a black suit, was mostly bald, and always friendly. There was no motor sound when the elevator moved up and down.

Arthur said these were full English breakfasts. He had ordered them without smoked fish, but sometimes added porridge, which was really just oatmeal. The bacon was very thick, tasty, and meaty, not quite crisp and never burned. It was just toasted on the edges. There were curled butterballs and marmalade along with toast and rolls. And today, fluffy scrambled eggs, and, always, tea for all. Milk, sugar cubes, and strong tea from India. India used to be a British colony for a long time, and English people still owned the plantations where the tea was grown. There were orange slices and melons, too. They called it Spanish Melon, and it was so ripe and sweet!

Breakfast was always my favorite meal. I never had leftovers on my plate except for the parsley. Chris always ate everything on his plate, too, even the parsley, which was placed next to the eggs on the breakfast plates just for show. He usually took the parsley from my plate and Duncan's plate and chewed it up, everything except the stem. I tried that but it tasted bitter. I guess it is actually a vegetable.

Mary came in after a few minutes and gave Duncan and me a snuggle from behind before she sat down. She was just having tea and one piece of toast. Sometimes, when we would go away overnight on vacation, she would eat more, but not on these library workdays. She had her briefcase all ready, leaned up next to the door.

October 8 – Getting to Know Chris

It was Monday again, so back to our school lessons, on the fourth floor of the Old St. James House, which is what we would call the fifth floor at home. The Old St. James House had many guests who stayed for months or even years. We saw the same people in the elevator each day when we went out. After breakfast, the trolley was wheeled away into the hallway next to the elevator, so we could turn the dining room area into our school room.

We were having fun getting to know Chris. He seemed to like us okay. He teased me a lot and played small tricks on us. He looked after us from eight-thirty in the morning, after breakfast, until almost dinner time, for lessons and then outings. He also took us on outings or out for lunch sometimes, and also on weekends if our parents had somewhere they had to go to meet people.

Chris was from Boston, which he called "The Hub of the Universe," or the "Hub" for short. It did not seem to matter to him that Boston was smaller than New York, London, or Tokyo. I don't know how I knew this because I had never been to Boston. Anyway, he went to Roxbury Latin School in Boston, had worked summers writing for *The Boston Globe*, went to Yale, where he answered an ad looking for a tutor, and he smoked Camels. This was his first trip beyond New England. Both of our parents smoked, too. Mary liked L&M, and Arthur preferred unfiltered Chesterfields.

I had told Chris he should stop smoking. He said he would if I stopped biting my nails. So I had been trying really hard. One nibble by me was one cigarette for him. If a whole nail was bitten off, he called it "demolition job," and Chris got a whole pack. If I stopped even for a few days, he would be really worried. Unlike Mary's cigarettes, Camels had no filter, so very often Chris had to pick off or spit out a little piece of tobacco from his lips or tongue. Arthur also smoked unfiltered cigarettes. Two fingers on each of Arthur's hands were stained brown, and so were his teeth.

October 11 – The Queen Opens Parliament

We have been in London for about three weeks. The opening of Parliament happens every year at about this time, and we went down to the wide mall to watch the Queen in her carriage as part of a long parade.

Our hotel sat at the end of a small side street called Saint James Place, and when we walked out this morning we turned right. First, we passed St. James Palace with its wide courtyard set in among other stone and brick buildings. This is where a woman named Queen Elizabeth the Queen Mother lived. She was actually and really the queen's mother, and her husband was the King of England before Elizabeth, but then he died.

I begged Chris not to make a scene, but he had started these antics (Mary's word) a few days before, of greeting the Queen Mother whenever we walked by. He stood apart and waved his hands and shouted, "Hi Lizzie!" while blowing kisses. It was really awful. Luckily, the guards, in red coats and huge bear hats, holding their muskets, ignored him.

The Queen's carriage on its way to Parliament

It was sunny all day, and while we waited by the road, the parade began with stately and huge Rolls Royce cars and limousines, and uniformed men on horseback. They were all dressed up in their special uniforms with medals and sashes. Arthur explained that the order of the parade was carefully arranged ahead of time, according to tradition and rank, building up to the Queen and her footmen. She came by with her matched set of four horses stepping along "smartly," as they say here.

The Queen's husband, Prince Philip, who is a good sailor and sails Dragons, which are an Olympic sailing class, was sitting next to her and looked just like a prince was supposed to look, I suppose. He was handsome, smiled pleasantly, and looked a little bored. Or maybe that was just his "calm" face. I had my camera ready, and I think I got a good picture of her with him behind her, and how she waved her hand, which she has to do a lot. She turned it on her wrist like screwing and unscrewing a light bulb, back and forth, but not waving like we do.

Afterwards, we walked a different way back to the Old St. James House. I was glad Chris wouldn't be able to act up for the second time that day. Whew!

We passed a building that was all piled up in broken pieces of stone, brick, and metal on the ground. Mary explained how during the war the Germans bombed London every night for months. No one in London was allowed to turn on any lights, for fear of attracting the bombers. Her father, our Grandpa Sam, who was a Colonel in the U.S. Army, had been in London during the bombing, which was called The Blitz. It had been 17 years since the end of the war, but there was still lots of work to do to rebuild. The fallen buildings looked like it could have happened just a few days before.

We stopped on the way back at a Lyons Corner House tea house for tea and a snack. They brought pots of tea to the table with the milk already in it. Just add sugar. Some tea spilled out of the spout when I poured, but nobody seemed to mind! I loved the strong, sweet taste of the tea, especially late in the afternoon when it was getting cooler and a little darker outside.

People were having sweet biscuits and rolls, and even small sandwiches with ham and cheese and mustard. British people had quite a large snack at about four or five in the afternoon, which they called "Tea." With extra goodies and sweets, it was called "High Tea." The British seemed to be eating pretty often, as Arthur explained it. First, there was breakfast, then "elevenses," then dinner at midday, about one o'clock. By late afternoon it was time for tea, like we had at the Lyons, and then supper was in the evening. So they ate five times a day.

As part of my snack, I had strawberry ice cream, because I had what my parents called a "sweet tooth." The ice cream did not taste at all like strawberries or cream. It tasted and smelled like floor polish or cleaner. And it was also kind of grainy.

It was cool outside by the time we left the Lyons; outside, the leaves were still mostly green on the trees.

October 12 – **Simpson's in the Strand**

YESTERDAY WAS THE FIRST DAY since we got to London that it was really raining hard even before it was light outside, so we stayed home in the afternoon and did more lessons to get ahead. Chris read to us from A Tale of Two Cities sometimes in the afternoon, and also every night at bedtime. The book was written about London and Paris by Charles Dickens. It had some very scary parts. It helped that Chris put a Shilling in the heater and the living room got a lot warmer.

Two nights before we had gone to a Spanish restaurant that our parents really liked. It had a covered courtyard in the middle with beautiful rust-and-yellow-colored tiles and also blue and green tiles on the floor. They had lots of rice dishes with tomatoes, and Mary liked the fish. Duncan and I had chicken and salad with fresh tomatoes.

Last night, though, we had an extra special treat. We went to Simpson's in the Strand. The Strand is a road in the center of London where banks and many other offices were, and also many theaters.

For this we had to wear our dress clothes including our blue ties, blazers, and Bermuda shorts with knee socks. Arthur said it was required.

We walked in and I looked up. The ceilings were huge and curved with gold moldings and painted leaves. The carpet was dark green with gold rope designs in a square pattern, but very soft colors. The curtains must have been 15 feet tall, dark green velvet, and the brass chandeliers hung in two rows. Arthur said it was just the way it had been when he was in college back in 1936.

The tables were round and far apart so no one could hear other people. I think we were the noisiest ones, because a couple of times a white-haired man at the next table turned around and looked over his gold-rimmed glasses at me, without smiling at all, and then kept his eyebrows raised as he looked at the white-haired woman next to him.

Anyway, roast beef was their specialty. Mary had calves liver with onions, bacon, and gravy. She does not like rare red meat and does not eat chicken. Once when she was a child in Alabama, she had a pet chicken who annoyed the cook. So, one day he cooked it and served it for dinner and that was the end of eating chicken for her for the rest of her life.

The waiters wore white coats and brought our food on big silver trolleys with silver wheels and spokes. First, the huge roast, which was carved at the table after the waiter made a show of sharpening the long knife. My piece filled almost two-thirds of my plate. Then came fresh Yorkshire pudding, which was puffy and crisp, with beef au jus, also a house specialty. It was thicker than just meat juice, but not as thick as gravy, as explained to me. Just right, I thought. And peas with teeny, tiny, boiled onions, and plenty of butter. My, it was good!

The vanilla cake, with five layers, had chopped fresh oranges and strawberries and whipped cream in between. It was tasty, but nothing could beat the roast beef!

It was still raining after dinner, maybe even a little harder, so we took a cab home. It was an Austin diesel cab, with three seats across the back for the grown-ups, and two smaller folding seats for Duncan and me, just like the ones we rode in coming from the airport. Arthur said they were just about the same as the ones he remembered from when he was a student at Oxford University in 1936 and 1937, 25 years ago.

October 15 – The Norfolk Broads

INSIDE THE FRONT OF OUR COPY of *Swallows and Amazons*, by Arthur Ransome, one of my favorite books, there was a map of the lakes and rivers where the stories took place. But it was not until Mary mentioned traveling to the Norfolk Broads that I realized that those were actual places, not just made up for the books.

Saturday's trip was planned, and we took an early train to Norfolk from Liverpool Street Station. London had many different train

Chris, Mary, and Jonny in the launch, Norfolk Broads

stations depending on which direction you wanted to go. Once we were out into the country, the train tracks curved through fields and along lakes and little ponds, passing small dams and lots of small boats pulled up in marshes. Here and there a sail hung limp. Everything was still, quiet, and very flat.

When we got off at the Norfolk Station along with only a few other people, we walked along the waterfront, and Arthur suggested tea and a snack at a thatched roofed inn. It was nice to sit down outside in the quiet, even though we had just been sitting on the train.

Duncan and I had hot chocolate and several bites of a delicious apple turnover with powdered sugar all over it. Mary had tea, and then a crunchy bun with raisins and nuts that she smeared with lots of butter. Not her usual, but she was relaxed and smiling and also dropping lots of crumbs which pigeons were watching carefully.

The Old Saint James House had packed us a picnic of ham and cheese sandwiches for later, which Mary carried in her huge bag.

It was chilly so we had our coats buttoned all the way up, as the North Sea was not far away, and the water there was very cold.

Along the quay there were lots of small boats tied up, including some sailboats and rowing skiffs. A man was sitting next to a motorboat smoking a pipe, and he offered to take us on a boat tour. Our parents thought this was a great idea, so we hopped aboard.

The man showed Duncan and me how to untie the boat and then steer it. He let us steer a little when we were away from land. We motored slowly past farmhouses, villages, and a few fishermen here and there. The motor chugged away, and Mary sat in the way back, smiling almost the whole time. She liked the close-by smell of salt water and the calm country setting, too.

I knew our parents were working hard at the archives and libraries during the week, and it was probably very dusty in those rooms with no windows. So, weekend trips were something we all looked forward to. It was a break from American history for me, European history for Duncan, and Chinese history for our parents.

We finished our paper-wrapped sandwiches on the boat. Arthur said it was Cheshire cheese in the sandwiches. He liked to say, "Dig in, French style," but nobody knew what that actually meant. Maybe we would find out when we went to France, but Mary doubted it. Whatever it was, the sandwiches were good and at just the right time. English butter was also really good and creamy, and there was plenty of that on the sandwiches, along with a few slices of cucumber and a few drops of mustard.

There were two boys working on a small skiff, a flat-bottomed rowboat, in the marsh, and we waved to them. They waved back and could have been right out of one of the Arthur Ransome stories like Swallowtail, big rubber boots and all.

We headed back to the dock and to the train so we could get back to London before dark. We had seen a lot in the last two hours, and I felt quiet. No traffic noise, none of Chris's antics! I felt calm and sleepy. Being on the water does that to me. When we got back to London, the taxi driver had to take us on a route that went around Picadilly Circus, which seemed like a good name, with all the people and cars everywhere.

October 22 – **Punting in Cambridge**

Dingy rowing to prepare for punting

WE HAD BEEN DOING LESSONS for at least four hours every morning, and some days until two o'clock in the afternoon. Soon, Chris needed to send our tests to the homeroom teachers at the Calvert School in Baltimore, so we had to get ready, and get as far ahead as we could.

But on Saturday, we went to Cambridge to see the town and the university there. There are beautiful courtyards and gates and gardens, and lots of stone buildings! It was sunny and warm for this time of year. Actually, it had not rained that much while we had been here, so far. People talked about the rain all the time, but there had not been that much.

Arthur knows other history scholars at Cambridge, so he went off to have lunch with them, but the rest of us, Mary, Chris, Duncan, and I, rented two punts on the river.

The water was completely still and was really just a canal. Lots of ducks, and very low bridges. Students were standing on the bridges, watching the ducks, watching the few girls that were walking around, talking, and smoking.

A punt is a small, square-bow, flat-bottom shallow barge. You put a pole in over the side and walk it back to the stern to push the boat forward. The man at the dock kept telling us that if we pushed too hard, the pole would go too deep in the mud and would not come out.

He said one boy our age did that and was left hanging off the end of his pole over the open canal. But it was really shallow, so I guess when he stopped yelling his head off, he just dropped into the water and waded to shore.

For us, when we came to a bridge, after one last push, we had to put the pole onto the boat and sit down low on the seats so we could slide under. There were spooky echoes in there, water slowly dripping from above, and shadowy fish slowly turning in the dark water.

We went out for lunch after we brought the punts back to the dock, and had sliced chicken sandwiches with lettuce, mayonnaise, and tomatoes, and chocolate milk to drink. Mary had a salad plate, which was basically the same but with more tomatoes and the bread on the side. Chris and Mary each had a beer with their lunches and seemed relaxed. I liked it a lot when we had these quiet times with one of our parents.

It was bright and sunny, so we sat outside in front of the restaurant and slowly sipped our hot chocolate. Chris had coffee to finish off his lunch. Almost everyone smoked there, even while eating.

October 23 – White Shirts, Blue Pants, Red Blood

WE HAD BEGGED OUR PARENTS to have Chris take us to the Royal London Automobile Show, and today we went! Duncan and I were interested in cars, and so was Arthur. Chris had planned for us to take two different buses to get there because it was pretty far from where we lived.

When we were on the second bus, there was a sudden swerve and then a gasp from the other riders as the bus stopped suddenly.

I looked out the right side and saw a black man in a white shirt and black pants lying on the road. His head was up on the curb. His pant leg was torn open, and his leg inside was cut open and there was a lot of blood.

Some people on the bus muttered that he was doing what they called "jaywalking," and was not crossing in the right place, like it was his fault. I felt really bad because people were standing around and his family was crying, including his daughter who was about my age.

Arthur had explained that the British were very accepting of people from their colonies like Barbados and Antigua, but nothing seemed friendly about this. The bus driver was talking with a policeman. Nobody was in a hurry. The man was still lying in the road. What if he lost that leg or he died? What would happen to his children and their mother?

I knew I would remember the white shirt, blue pants, red blood, and black face like that for my whole life. Chris quickly got us off the bus, turned right and then left around the corner, and away from all the people who were standing around. We walked the rest of the way.

The show was at a place called Earl's Court, all covered over, and full of all the new cars ready for the 1963 automobile season. Their names were Morris, Vauxhall, Austin, Morgan, and more. There were French cars, too, including a Citroën with a very different shape. Duncan called it an anteater, but I thought maybe more of a spaceship. There was also a Mercedes sedan from Germany.

There was a Rolls Royce with doors that opened from the middle, like house doors, with lots of beautiful wood and red leather inside. A man who stood by the door wore white gloves and did not allow anyone inside. But we could look. This particular model had additional folding seats in front of the rear seats. Chris called them jump seats, like ones we have seen before, I guess for children like Duncan and me. They were a lot nicer than the ones in Austin cabs. Really, they were huge full-sized seats with wood trim and red leather, like something a person would have in their living room.

Another man had a soft cloth and was constantly moving around the car to make sure it was shiny and spotless. Really well-dressed people in suits and fancy dresses, and with cigarette holders, were walking slowly around the car, gesturing, talking to other rich people, and pretending not to be interested.

Farther on, there was the new model Chevrolet Corvette Stingray, sparkling silver with a ridge down the top part of its back that made room for a couple of very small seats in the back, so it was called a "two plus two." It was really cool! The hood was open and everything shone inside. The salesman here had on a shirt with silver snap buttons and a string tie with a buffalo head on it. He had no jacket and he was smoking.

There was also a dark green sports car called a Morgan which had an older style to it, with a long engine cover in front, and a leather strap and buckle over the cover, which is called a bonnet here, not a hood. It only had two seats. It was like an MG, but much cooler and longer. The salesman explained that it had a wooden frame made of ash wood that could flex and bend over rough roads. The wheels had individual spokes kind of like a bicycle.

The salesman told us the car only had an oiled canvas top, and beautiful brown leather inside, all stitched by hand. He was dressed in a nice jacket that Chris identified as Harris Tweed, with a matching cap and white mustache to blend; he said the Morgan could do 115 miles per hour. I asked him if he could start the engine so I could hear it, but he said no. We also walked around and saw the newest Minis and a Morris Estate Wagon with real wood paneling on the outside.

Then Chris made us walk home. All the way. He liked to walk and said it was good for us to see the city from the same level as everyone else. But most of them are a lot taller than I am. It was so far and took hours and hours. I was finally so tired that I began complaining, and Chris said not to whine. Once he told me to go soak my head in the toilet and pull the chain, but he was smiling. The toilets in London had tanks up on the wall with chains so he was not kidding, and that was a LOT of water.

The worst of it though, after he started that thing with greeting the Queen Mother at her place near our hotel, was that today he started teasing me by pretending to carry a huge piano over his head down the sidewalk. Everyone was watching. Even a policeman looked at him for a moment. Maybe he was going to help us? Chris just did not know how tired I was, and it was not very funny at all. Duncan did not like it, either, but he did not complain. He is older than I am anyway.

I was still scared about the man who was hit by the bus. I hoped I wouldn't have too many bad dreams about that.

October 31 – Churches, Castles, Dungeons

Manning the drawbridge!

OVER THE LAST TWO WEEKS, we had seen a lot of churches, cathedrals, and also one or two prisons. I started writing this as a theme assignment for Chris. It seemed like all we had been doing, when not doing our lessons, was going to forts and churches.

From where we lived in London we could walk to the Underground station, so we took the Underground, also called the "tube," and got off at Westminster Station where parliament had their meetings. We also saw the Big Ben clock and tower and Westminster Abbey, the biggest church in London and the place where kings and queens were christened, married, crowned, and buried.

The Abbey had a beautiful courtyard with grass on the right side and covered walks around the outside where the monastery had been, and where I think priests and monks used to live. The inside of the Abbey was very ornate and detailed with stone carvings and lots of dark, ancient wood. Still, I was surprised by how light it was inside even on a cloudy day. The clear, light-colored glass high up let in light that flickered down the stone columns and walls onto the polished floor. Many of the floor stones were about the size of a person, and that was because famous people were actually buried there under my feet.

The other really big church in London was Saint Paul's Cathedral, which was designed by Sir Christopher Wren and had a beautiful dome rather than tall spires. It is made of white stone. We had ridden by on a double-decker bus, but next week there was a visit planned, I think.

Last Saturday we went to Canterbury and Dover. Mary explained that Canterbury Cathedral was the main church for the archbishop of all Episcopalians. That was the religion set up by Henry VIII so he could get a divorce. It was also the church that we went to at home, but not that often.

Canterbury was a huge cathedral with big, beautiful windows, and more carved wood and stone. We also went to Dover and had lunch and looked at the white cliffs from the pier. The cliffs were made of chalk, which is a rock, a lot like what teachers used in school on blackboards, and the cliffs were so white that sailors could see them from miles away, even in bad weather.

We have visited a lot of palaces, dungeons and forts. Last week we visited another castle with a moat and drawbridge to get to the front gate. It had an iron grate called a portcullis that dropped down to keep out invaders and bandits. The whole castle was made of rough stone.

Early Christian church ruins, Canterbury

The dungeon was off to the left side and had a stone in the floor that moved. It was called a "tilt stone." When they wanted to kill someone, they had him stand on the stone, and it had an iron pin in it, so it hinged. The prisoner fell through the floor into the moat below. There was an iron grate out to the main moat, but it did not open. The prisoner would have screamed and cried and then drowned. I had really wanted to see this but also it was really scary. I could almost see that guy there and it was so horrible.

We also visited the Tower of London, where many tortures and executions were held, usually for the public to watch. I have had nightmares about this huge roller wheel with spikes sticking out all over. The prisoner was strapped on to the slowly turning wheel, and as it rolled the prisoner was speared through all over many times.

Arthur reminded us that our family had English roots and relatives, and he also reminded us of the many museums and universities that were also part of the country and its history, as well as many achievements. Mary told us that he was an "anglophile." Not me, at least not the torture part.

When the queen wanted to get away from all the palace work, the noise, and the soot, she would take Prince Philip and their children to Windsor Castle, which was close to London. It was one of several of her castles that she liked to visit. The chapel there was a lot smaller than in the really big churches and cathedrals, but it was a peaceful space and just the right size for a small group or big family. Outside the castle buildings, but inside the walls and gates, there were other houses where the queen's sisters and other family members lived.

She had already been the queen for ten years, so she had been the queen for my whole life so far. Her name was on almost everything. Letters were delivered by the Royal Mail, which was their post office. You could mail letters in the bright red mailboxes that were on many street corners. They were made of iron, and said 'ER II' on them, which stood for Elizabeth Regina the Second. Some still said 'GR VI' for George Rex the Sixth, her father. He was the king when Arthur was at Oxford. His widow was Queen Elizabeth the Queen Mother, who lived at Saint James Palace near where we lived, and where Chris made me want to run and hide whenever we walked by. Imagine if she really was looking out toward the street when he started blowing kisses!

November 4 – I Hate Dr. No!

LAST SATURDAY we had been invited to go out to lunch at the American Ambassador's residence in London. Our parents seemed to know Ambassador David Bruce and assured us that the Bruces had a son about our age, and we would have fun.

When we got there, the taxi dropped us off under the huge columned entryway, which must have been at least 15 feet tall. Two men in dark blue jackets, white gloves, and very well-polished shoes opened the doors of our smelly Austin cab, and they nodded silently to our parents as they leaned forward and pulled themselves out using the hand straps. One of the men offered Mary a gloved hand and she took it, though she hardly needed it.

Inside, the building was really ornate, with polished wood floors, shiny brass lighting on the walls, large paintings of the English countryside, and the ambassador and his family were there to greet and welcome us.

The place had nothing American about it at all. Mr. Bruce was very nice, and Mrs. Bruce stayed off to the side, smiling. I think Mr. Bruce and Arthur were in college together, but I was not sure. Anyway, they were happy to see each other. Arthur's blue eyes always got very sparkly and bright when he greeted old friends.

Nicky Bruce was older than even Duncan. We walked around the patio before it started raining and I tried to think of things to say. He seemed to be waiting for something to happen. I think he was told by his parents to be with us and to keep us company, so I guess he was our ambassador.

When it was time for lunch we went into the dining room. I had been thinking we might be having sandwiches in the kitchen with the family and then maybe play checkers or something, but no such luck. This table easily seated 30, so we all clustered on both sides in the middle with white linen everywhere. Remember, this was just a Saturday lunch with friends.

The chairs were carved wood, which blended with the carved ceiling and wall details, including the molding around the swinging French doors out to the patio. The ceiling was painted a creamy white color with a few gold and green touches here and there. We had some French doors on our sunporch at home, but not like these, which were at least ten feet tall and curved at the top. The glass was a little wavy, too.

Nicky sat between us as we waited for food and listened to the grown-ups talk and laugh. Mrs. Bruce and Mary were served first, and Mary exclaimed: "Oh boy, calves' liver!" She liked liver, but my heart sank like a rock. She looked down toward us with a very slight smile and tipped her head to the side, and that helped a little. The plates came empty at first but hot, and there was the full golden seal of the United States, eagle and all, right there in front of me. Then the waiters came and put creamed spinach on the plate and then the liver, topped with a creamy sauce with mushrooms from a silver dish with a spout. I hated spinach anyway and this was really soggy. And never mind the liver. I just sat and looked away.

About this time, Mr. Bruce announced that Nicky would be taking us boys to a new movie after lunch, called *Dr. No*. They all seemed to know about James Bond and that it was an adventure movie.

I looked to the side when the waiter took the plate away, where I had just pushed the food around to make it look a little messy. We left as soon as we were allowed, and we took a cab with Nicky. The movie started right away being really scary, with lots of spooky scenes in the dark with gunfire and people being shot. I kept reminding myself that it was a movie, but it was so real that I just could barely stand it.

I got up and went to the bathroom and when I was just coming back, something happened in the movie where the girl screamed, and lots of people in the theater screamed, and I screamed, too, and covered my eyes. I had to walk around in the dark without looking at the screen to find my seat with Duncan and Nicky. I really did not understand who Dr. No was, and what exactly had happened. I could not wait for it to be over. Even though Nicky had told us that everything always worked out in the end for the agent named James Bond, that really did not help me very much.

The cab ride back to the St. James House was filled with Nicky's excitement over the movie. He talked to Duncan mostly, who was as always polite, and seemed to have understood the story better than I had. I thanked him for taking us. Or I meant to, anyway.

Once we got back, we went up to our suite and I went into our bedroom and closed the door. That was three days ago, and each night has been terrible. Each day had been a regular day with school-work, but I could not get those pictures of the people being shot out of my head. They kept coming back every time I closed my eyes.

November 11 – Rain in the Cotswolds

YESTERDAY, SUNDAY, we were off to an early start after breakfast and got back to our rooms late for a cold supper of chicken, ham, and tongue. The day started cold and wet and stayed that way except for a little sunshine just before lunch. We went by car and driver into the Cotswolds region where there were lots of villages with stone cottages, farmhouses, and sheep everywhere.

On our route for the day, too, was Oxford University, where Arthur went to university for a year after he finished college. He studied Buddhism, the Japanese tea ceremony, and other religious practices and traditions while he was there.

I could tell he really liked the place, even with its cramped and damp rooms and the terrible food back then that he had told us about. Arthur got all smiley and was full of big grins, which showed a few of his teeth that were repaired with gold. And also, the spaces for the missing ones. It was fun to see him happy. Sometimes he could get going with silly jokes and was really funny. I liked to do stuff that made him smile and laugh. I never knew what would "tickle his fancy," as he said, so I tried all sorts of different things.

He lived at University College, known as Univ. As soon as we got there and began walking around, he started speaking with a bit more of his British accent, which did not seem to bother anyone except Duncan and me.

I wish I could remember the driver's name for sure. I think it was Daniel. English people use the full name for grown-ups, not "Dan." I usually remember everything. Anyway, the car was a polished black Daimler limousine with beautiful wood on the door panels and dashboard, and red leather inside. It reminded me of the Auto Show at Earl's Court. It had a folding middle row of red leather seats for Duncan and me, much bigger than the jump seats in the Austin cabs, but not as fancy as the Rolls Royce at the show. The seats could fold up against the back of the front seats, but when unfolded they were about two-thirds the size of a regular seat, which was just right for Duncan and me.

Mary and Chris rode in the big back seats, and Arthur and the driver were up front. Arthur would turn around to give us his comments as we rolled through the hills and farms. He explained that Daimler was the British "cousin" of the German-made Mercedes. During the war, he explained, they became separate companies. Daimlers, along with Bentleys and Rolls Royces, were the choice of British royalty and rich people, except for the queen's husband Prince Philip who preferred Jaguars and his Land Rover. The queen also drove her own Land Rover sometimes when staying at one of her castles.

We stopped at an old inn in one of the villages for lunch. It had a thatched roof and a very low doorway, so even I had to duck a little. Inside it smelled of wood smoke; the big open fireplace was very warm and cozy. We sat right next to it and had grilled ham and cheese sandwiches. Thick slabs of ham and cheddar cheese were all melted and toasted. Most people were having their main Sunday meal, and so the smells of roasted potatoes and roast beef and mutton were everywhere.

Back outside I could still smell the wood smoke in the air and on my sweater. In this valley where we had stopped, there were stone walls and wooden gates everywhere, with sheep, goats, and cows that wandered around in green pastures. The hillsides were not too steep but disappeared quickly up into the clouds on both sides.

Daniel and his Daimler

Duncan and Jonny spying for treats

It was beginning to get darker when we started back for London, and it was raining hard again. Once we got on the main highways, the roads were more crowded and had a middle lane used by drivers in both directions, but just for passing. Our driver was very calm and skilled with his car, and he reassured us that he had not put "a scratch on her in 20 years."

I could see up through the windshield as the wipers slowly moved back and forth. Water gushed up over the bonnet or hood. Other car lights shone off the wet roads.

When the speedometer began creeping up over 100 miles per hour and our driver was traveling mostly in the middle passing lane, Mary's fists were white and tightly gripping the armrests. She does not like cars much anyway, and this speeding in the rain and dark, which was supposed to be a quiet end to a luxurious Sunday drive, was not helping at all.

Chris looked out the window on the left side, as the passing cars sprayed walls of water up onto the side of the Daimler.

Arthur leaned over and said something to the driver, and I could hear his reply "Oh, it's quite all right, sir. She'll do 140!" Mary had taken to looking out the right-side windows into the black and rain. I did not know what to look at and just wanted to be home. As we got closer to London, there were more cars, traffic, and intersections slowing us down. Whew!

We went all the way down to a slow crawl around Piccadilly Circus. Once the car stopped, we made a final dash from the Daimler to the front door of the Old St. James House, where the smell of wet wool was everywhere. The cold supper was waiting for us in our rooms. Arthur had also ordered hot tea, which was just right for us, while our mother and he had martinis.

November 18 – A Beagling Weekend

WE WENT FOR THE WEEKEND to the small brick country house of friends of somebody, maybe of the ambassador, and we stayed overnight two nights in Kent. Duncan and I were the only children.

On Saturday, beagling was the big adventure. I knew a little bit about these dogs, but this was a whole outing with horses, special uniforms, and lots of calling and barking. The men had leather pants and were "running the hounds." It seemed we, or they, were using the dogs to find rabbits or foxes, and we were to be careful not to fall into the animals' holes. I guess it was basically just hunting. The grown-up men were on their horses off somewhere up ahead. We chased the dogs where we thought they were, through the vines and thorns and brambles, and I listened to the barking get farther and farther away. One or two shots were fired, at least that was all we heard.

I was so glad when it was time to go back to the guesthouse and have lunch and sit by the fire. Mary cleaned up our many scratches from thorns and put on bright orange mercurochrome and Band-Aids. I sort of liked getting dirty and being outside, but I never understood what we were doing that day, and why. Our parents were full of questions about the beagling, but I did not have many answers. They seemed to have enjoyed their time outside bundled up in the cool morning air drinking lots of tea.

Sunday morning came just in time for an English breakfast. We had poached eggs, grilled ham, smoked bacon, roasted potatoes, sausage, and toast. Smoked fish and kippered something were offered to our parents, and some kind of hard sausage-like thing, too. There was plenty of tea and chunky marmalade on buttered toast to make a feast for us!

Jonny and Duncan with the friendly hound, Kent

We were back in London by late Sunday afternoon, and the nice evening waiter at the St. James House brought up our usual Sunday cold supper of chicken, ham, and tongue. He had a silver trolley cart with food on top, and plates, silver, and linens below. When he came, he and the elevator man Brian, pushed it out of the elevator.

The waiter said almost nothing other than polite greetings to our parents as he laid out the meats, the sliced tomatoes and cucumbers, and the toast. Our parents had their mixed drinks, and we had cold water to drink. It had been a long trip back by train from Kent and it was getting colder. I was tired.

Last week, Brian had noticed that we had new flat caps to go with our double-breasted coats because the weather was getting colder, and he said, "Jolly nice cheese cutters, boys!" I liked Brian.

We had gotten the caps in a market in the East End of London where there were all kinds of games, fortune telling, art and trinkets, as well as pets for sale. I really liked meeting the parrots and listening to them talk. I got my picture taken holding a monkey, and with a parrot on my head. Arthur looked amused in the picture. I think he liked my joking around, at least sometimes.

Earlier last week, Arthur said that a truck would be coming in a few days to take all our books in their big blue trunk to the docks for shipping. We were almost at the end of our London time. I was really liking the city.

Holland

Laundry day on the canal

November 23 – Windmills and Wooden Shoes

Hotel Krasnapolsky on the Dam

It was cloudy and cold outside when we woke up in Amsterdam on our second morning. There was steam on the window glass, dripping down to the bottom. We watched bicycles go back and forth along the canal while we ate breakfast. We were staying at the Hotel Krasnapolsky in the middle of the city, and it faced toward the main plaza (called the Dam) on one side and toward one of the canals on the other side.

The food was very different than in London. The breakfast table was set with cups and plates, and the waiter brought a basket of rolls and bread. There was a plate of curled butter balls on the table, as well as pots of jam and jelly. White tablecloths and napkins were everywhere. Tall windows looked out onto the main plaza, where people were walking briskly with their scarves and hair blown about by the wind off the ocean.

The bread was warm in the basket, and the special rolls were very flaky and unfolded and unrolled in our hands. The butter melted quickly inside and then on went the jam! These were really delicious, and Duncan and I helped ourselves as we have each morning here. The waiter brought a second basket, and then a third, as Chris had taken a liking to the hard rolls, and Mary to the sweet bread.

Mary said that these curved buttery rolls were a specialty of France and part of a "continental" breakfast. There was also a side plate of wedges of ham and a creamy yellow Dutch cheese called Gouda, which Arthur liked a lot. Duncan said it tasted very "gooda," which we both thought was very funny. We were on the continent of Europe now and this was what they ate. No bacon or eggs. But my, these were good, and the hot chocolate was creamy and piping hot.

The other side of the open lobby looked out over a canal where a small barge was motoring slowly. Along the canal, two other barges were tied up next to the sidewalk, and I saw people moving around on the narrow side decks getting ready for their day. It looked like they were having rolls and coffee with wisps of steam rising from the cups. They were gesturing back and forth with some people stopped on bicycles.

There were so many bicycles, four or five next to each other going down the busy streets! The street was busy because of the bicycles and also taxis and buses. There were people going to work with briefcases strapped on the back of their bicycles, and older children in uniforms on their way to school.

Yesterday, I really liked seeing the dikes and seawalls that hold the ocean back, and the brown fields that were used to grow the famous Dutch tulips in the spring. I liked thinking of the colors, even though they weren't there. We went to see a working wooden windmill with canvas sails. Two of the four panels were open and the other two were furled, and it was turning slowly. The windmills were used to pump out water and keep away the sea because part of the country was below the ocean level at high tide.

I got some hand-carved wooden shoes that were painted red around the bottom and had tiny flowers painted on the toes, which turned up a little.

France

November 24 – Needle and Thread!

THE TRIP TO THE AMSTERDAM AIRPORT was short the next morning. Once at the airport, there was still time for a last cup of Dutch hot chocolate. We flew to Paris on a KLM Lockheed Electra propeller plane. It was a turbo-prop, which Arthur tried to explain to me. The engines made a whirring and whining sound and were very smooth. The stewardesses had on light blue suits, striped light and dark blue scarves, and hats with KLM pins.

When we arrived at the Paris airport there were some delays getting luggage and going through customs at Le Bourget Airport. It took quite a long time, and our parents spoke some French but not a lot. It was different, I guess, reading French in a library, and then trying to speak to a person in a uniform who had a frown on their face.

Outside the airport we were to be met by a scholar and friend of Arthur's who teaches Chinese history at the Sorbonne University in Paris, but he was not there. Soon after, he arrived, full of apologies. We had flown into Le Bourget airport, not the new Orly airport, so he had to come back here for us. Etienne Balasz was wearing a suit and was quite bald. He was really happy to see us and greeted Mary with a slight dip of the head and cheek-to-cheek kiss greeting. That does not happen in England.

Three of us were in Professor Balasz's car, and the others followed in a taxi with the luggage. His car, he explained, was the new Citroën model that was becoming more popular, replacing the old and much-loved Deux Chevaux. His car had more comfortable seats and was called the Trois Chevaux. Arthur and Mr. Balasz, whom he called

Etienne, discussed some of the finer points of the improved car, and also that their German friend in Munich very much preferred English cars. Neither of them understood why because they always broke down—they smiled and shook their heads about poor Hans.

Coming to our hotel, our cars turned off the Boulevard St. Germain onto a small side street called Rue St. Simon, then into a small courtyard. The hotel was an old building with ivy growing up the walls and around the windows, and a sign over the door that said, "Hôtel Saint Simon," with a little "hat" over the "o" in hotel.

It was pretty dark inside the small lobby, but the madame was very welcoming and so polite. We would be staying for a month. Mr. Balasz translated that dinner would be available at seven. That was early for France, he noted, but the madame knew that we were traveling with children, Duncan and me.

Duncan and I settled into our room and unpacked. He got two upper drawers, and I got the two lower drawers. I heard our parents in the next room discussing something. We could hear because the doors were open to the hall. Apparently, some shirt or pajama buttons had come loose. Arthur had asked at the desk, and then the madame called Mr. and Mrs. Balasz at their home miles away in the suburbs.

A needle and thread sewing kit were to be sent through the Metro tunnels in a vacuum tube called a "pneumatique." Then the package would arrive through the tube to the closest Metro station where a postman would pick up the package and deliver it to the hotel. It was expected to take thirty minutes at the most. I had never heard of this thing called a "pneumatique," but I think it was like the tube Arthur used for paying at Abercrombie and Fitch in New York.

The toilet for us to use was down the hall, with a huge tank up on the wall. It was used by all four rooms on this floor. We had a sink and bathtub in our own bathroom off the bedroom.

Dinner was just in time because I was really hungry, and Mary said I get "cross" when I get too hungry. When we gathered in the hotel dining room, I could see that there were about twelve tables, and we were assigned to two of them put together near the windows that looked onto the courtyard, which was paved with stone blocks. The floor carpet was greyish and faded, and the draperies were a soft green color. It was a quiet room. Each table had a small electric table lamp with a fringed shade near the wall or window side of the table.

Arthur ordered a bottle of red wine and quietly announced that French wine was the finest in the world. Then he explained that dinner was the chef's special or choice, the "table d'hôte" they called it. Everything was written out in nice handwriting on menus, but it was in French. Anyway, there wasn't any choice.

Dinner started with a "potage," which was soup made with potatoes, onion, parsley, and carrots and was thick, very tasty, and not too salty. I saw tiny flecks of different vegetables in the soup.

Then came the crispy-skinned roasted chicken with potatoes and a sauce with mushrooms, and green beans on the side. There was a salad afterward with a delicious lemon and mustard dressing. After the plates were taken away, the waiter brought a plate of cheese with apples for everyone. The meal was really good, especially the hard and flaky bread and soft butter.

Even if there had been a choice, this is the dinner I would have asked for. By the end I felt the opposite of "cross," which is happy and talking a lot. Our parents finished their wine, and Arthur told some stories about being in Paris as a student. Mary asked some questions, and he looked at her while tipping his head, and made vague answers about who some of his friends were. I think he left out some parts. Mary then looked at him a couple of times and maybe he winked once or twice.

For the rest of us, it was our first time here. Chris was quiet as he often was during dinner. I wondered if he missed his own family, being far from home and getting farther with each stop on this trip. I knew he sent postcards home almost every day.

November 28 – In the Huge Steel Cage

YESTERDAY WE HAD SOME MORNING LESSONS, mostly arithmetic and spelling, and Chris assigned us to write a theme. I just could not think of a topic, which made me worry, but I didn't cry. We went out for a snack and to see the Eiffel Tower, and then I knew I wanted to write about that adventure.

The tower was huge and almost 80 years old. It was designed by the same engineer who designed the inside structure that holds up New York's Statue of Liberty.

The tower began on widely spaced feet built like cages, and then slowly curved upward until it rose almost straight up. Even though it was very big, all the metal pieces were pretty small, like a giant erector set similar to the toy ones we had at home. Except our sets did not have any curved pieces.

Seine bridges from the Eiffel tower

From the bottom I could see the hundreds of steel steps going up through the legs and toward the main spire. We had to walk up because Chris said so, even though there was an elevator up through another of the legs. It went up at an angle to the main platform where there were some shops and binocular stands set up. You could put in a New Franc coin, which was 100 times as much money as the Old Franc, which was still around. That was confusing.

From the large platform above the main arch, we kept going up as far as we could go, to the second floor, but I really hated heights. Just the steel cage of thousands of bars and beams, and the steps with holes in them. Higher up, it started to be windier and colder. The weather was changing because it was almost December. I tightened the belt of my tan English coat. There was no place to go but up.

Once we got to the second floor, Chris wanted to go to the top of the spire, but not me. I liked looking out over the city on all four sides, and the ground was close enough that I could still see details of people and cars, even though they were really small.

When we got back down to the first floor, the big main level above the street level, we had a snack of a grilled sandwich called Croque Monsieur, which was ham and cheese with mustard on that same crunchy bread we had been having everywhere. We walked back toward the hotel through some gardens with reflecting pools with fountains that had been turned off for the winter. It started to rain a little. Taxi drivers leaned out their windows to see if we wanted a ride, but Chris ignored them. I knew by then to just keep walking and get home.

December 4 – Hôtel de Ville

LAST FRIDAY WAS A BIG DAY. The five of us were to take a weekend trip by car to the area around Beaune. We packed up our small bags and warm clothes, and Duncan and I had our BOAC green bags for books and a toothbrush and toothpaste. He had a hairbrush, but my haircut is called a modified butch, so I did not need one.

It started to drizzle while we waited in the courtyard of Hotel St. Simon for Arthur to return with the rental car, the first rental car of our trip. When the rain settled down onto Paris, the air smelled like smoke, and it was cold and there was dark smoke coming from the building chimneys.

The Citroën DS 19 sedan was maroon and had a tan cloth interior. We piled all the bags into the trunk and got in. Mary sat in front with Arthur, and I sat in the middle in the rear, with Chris on one side and Duncan on the other. Duncan promised to swap with me part way which was really nice. He watched out for me. But the middle was not bad at all because there was no hump in the rear seat or floor. These French cars drove with the front wheels instead of the back ones, so the floor was completely smooth. Arthur said other brands, too, like the tubby Panhard and the toy-like Renaults were made this way.

The back of the car was narrow while the front had a wide sloped hood. The turn signal lights were in tubes over the rear doors, very visible for drivers behind us, I think. Anyway, it was very comfortable and quiet even in the rain. Arthur commented that it had Michelin tires made right here in France.

It was pretty dark out by the time we got to Beaune. Mary had a good knowledge of French for reading signs, and she also had a map. The road signs were mostly round with pictures so even if you drove from Germany or Holland, you could still figure it out. The car swept along at about 90. But that was kilometers per hour so really not that fast.

Once in the town of Beaune, there was a large building on the left, which our parents said was the Hospices de Beaune, a famous hospital we would visit the next day. Just beyond it was a block of buildings on the right. A large one was brownstone on the outside and had a vertical green neon sign "Hôtel de Ville."

Arthur told us we would be staying here for two nights, as this was the main hotel for visitors to the town. He parked the Citroën next to the entrance and pushed a button to lift up the back of the car, so it was easier to get out. It was quiet inside the hotel, although a few people were gathering in the dining room and bar area to have drinks, and many were still in their outdoor or factory working clothes. Overhead there were round tubed bright lights that hummed. The whole room was painted pale green.

Upstairs our rooms had a shared bath with a tub on metal feet. I got under the bedspread for a while to warm up, until it was time for dinner.

Once we were downstairs again, Arthur quickly asked for the wine list, and the proprietor came with one, which was written by hand, and announced the meal for the evening, a potato and green onion soup, and beef stew in red wine and mushrooms, with potatoes. There were green beans with carrots also. And the bread would come right away. It all sounded good to me. This was France and the food was good!

While we waited for the food, Arthur tried to order a cocktail, a martini, which was his favorite. With an olive. The bartender looked very puzzled and brought over a bottle of Martini and Rossi vermouth, then various other items. Arthur seemed a little put out but settled for red wine. Other people in the room kept turning around and looking at us and I wanted to hide. I felt foreign and out of place.

The wine came and was from right here in Beaune, from three years ago, which was 1959, the same year that we moved from California to Connecticut. They tasted the wine and smiled, and everything seemed okay then.

Everything we ate tasted really fresh and not too salty. The waiter poured Duncan and me just a tiny bit of red wine with cold water added, while Arthur explained that French children our age brought a glass jar of wine and water to drink with lunch at school.

French people also liked their sweets, especially custards and chocolate. I had a crème custard with brown crusty sugar on top. Mary had several large bites and was pretending to be her father, Grandpa Sam, who was always really sneaky at stealing our ice cream. She wasn't as good at distracting us and doesn't like to steal, but she was very smiley while she ate some of my dessert, which I like. There was plenty for me, too.

Mary was usually very serious and thoughtful and also very observant and thinking about other people and what everyone else needed, so I was glad she could enjoy her sweets and be relaxed!

She also ate the stew, which she said was very good, even though she often said she did not like beef.

Chris had an espresso coffee with a lemon peel and sugar. Arthur had a cognac and then a little more cognac, and then it was time for bed. I think he was tired from driving and having to watch the road in the rain and darkness for so long.

December 5 – Guest House of God

Saturday morning in Beaune, we woke up kind of late because the room had dark curtains, and it was still raining outside. The hotel was quiet except for the sound of the big toilet tank flushing down the hall, in the little room that all of us used.

Going downstairs, the smells of fresh bread, cinnamon pastry, and coffee were soft and sweet. And something from last night's stew, maybe from some of the herbs, was still in the air, too. Breakfast for us was hot chocolate and lots of those flaky crescent-shaped rolls, along with some ham and cheese to put inside, in addition to the butter and jam.

Mary was looking forward to seeing the Hospices de Beaune. It was also called Hôtel Dieu, which means something like "Guest House of God." I really did not understand too much about why we were here before we came, except that we were in a famous wine area, so Mary tried to explain.

At the beginning, the Hospices had been the private house for a very rich man and then he converted it to be the first free hospital in France, especially for people who were really sick and had no money. It was also a special place for people who were not going to get better. The nuns took care of everyone there. This started nearly 450 years ago right here, during the Black Plague. I wondered if the nuns also got sick during that terrible plague, taking care of the other sick people.

We walked across the street and through the small square soon after breakfast. Starting with the really nice original big brick and stone farmhouse, the original buildings had been added onto many times. The roofs were covered with beautiful, patterned stone tiles, and there were old small-paned windows that pushed out in warm weather. A few were open today. There were faint smoke trails coming from a few of the chimneys.

Courtyard, Hospices du Beaune

There were gardens and plants and grass and benches everywhere around the courtyard and the buildings. A few roses were still climbing around the main arched entry to the courtyard, even in early December. Long ago, carts with sick patients and dead people passed in and out under this arch. Farmers with their fresh supplies have come and gone through this arch for centuries. The stones under my feet were rounded and smooth, and slippery from the rain.

Mary explained that providing the best care for people who have nothing else, and who are alone and sad, was a wonderful way of helping, especially if they were very poor or have no family. I think she hoped our country would do something like this. Being in the courtyard with our parents, all very quiet, gave me a safe and peaceful feeling.

After lunch at a café across the square from the hotel, we went to visit a winery. The concierge at the hotel had given Mary a map drawn on a piece of yellow paper. Clouds hung down over the hills just like they had in the Cotswolds. When we got there, we could see that all the grapes had already been taken off the vines because winter was coming.

The big barns had many barrels lying on their sides in racks. Most had dates marked on them in chalk or crayon. We heard that the older wines were in casks in a space partly underground where it would be cool in the summer and not as cold in the winter.

The wine from last year was ready for a first taste, and after one sip, our parents agreed that it was going to be very good, tipping their heads to the side slightly and nodding. This pleased the vineyard workers, and especially the main winemaker, who wore a white apron. For a snack they brought out wooden trays with fresh bread and special cheese made in a nearby town. Everyone was very friendly. I especially liked the smell of old wood in the barn and watching some goats and chickens scratching around and dancing.

Pretty soon it was time to go back to the hotel for dinner, so we all crammed back into the Citroën. I think our parents were okay speaking French but had very good manners, and French people always seemed polite. Chris spoke pretty good French, too, so we had been welcomed. Our parents were, as they liked to say, "feeling no pain," after tasting more than a sip or two of the many special wines.

December 6 – **Paris and the Marx Brothers**

Sunday, we went back to Paris from Beaune in the afternoon, and it was still raining off and on. By the time we got to the city, it was getting pretty dark and raining harder, and the streetlights glared off the shiny roads. We could barely see the people wrapped in black ponchos and jackets on the black Solex motorbikes riding along the side of the road. All they had was one tiny red light on the back that was much smaller than a flashlight. Their ponchos were pulled around their faces, so I didn't know how they could see anything at all.

Mary had to turn the map light on and off and was also trying to read the signs about how to get back to the Hôtel St. Simon. Quietly, I heard Arthur say, "I think we are going around the Etoile." Later Mary told us the word meant "star" in French. He sounded worried, which does not happen often. The Etoile was the road hub for all the main avenues in Paris and had the Arc de Triumph in the middle of it. It was like the huge turntables they use for trains, but this was even bigger, and cars were coming in and out of the five lanes very fast in the rain and dark. I think we left the Etoile as soon as possible and made our way somehow in the back streets.

Arthur was pretty quiet and did not get angry or upset very often. But I saw that his face was tired, and his eyes were very quiet, too, not as blue and sparkly as they usually were.

Then, on Monday, Arthur saw a notice that the Marx Brothers' movie *A Night at the Opera* with French subtitles was playing in the St. Germain area, not too far away. We were excited to go! Arthur loved these movies and also Laurel and Hardy where people throw pies at each other. Charlie Chaplin movies were another favorite of ours.

Anyway, we found the movie theater, got to our seats and waited. French people are pretty polite, as I have said before.

So, when Groucho said his funny and crazy things that have puns in them, Arthur would howl, Mary would chuckle, and then a few seconds later, the rest of the audience would laugh politely, but not before they had turned and stared at us. Mary tried to explain the French translations, but she said some of it really did not translate well. Of course, anyone could get Harpo's jokes because he never said anything at all, like when he would pull a hot cup of coffee out from under his raincoat with that funny stupid grin on his face.

They were both spending the days in the French Foreign Office records rooms, reading and photocopying documents for their Chinese history projects, so translating was a big part of their workdays.

At the archives, Mary was making many piles of photocopies of documents to send home. She told me that the copies will curl up, and that next summer when we get home, she will pay me to help her by wetting them and flattening them under her heavy books. She sure had plenty of those.

Anyway, it was good to laugh and to see our parents having fun. Chris enjoyed the Marx Brothers, too. We had dinner after the movie at a brasserie, and Arthur had better luck this time getting a martini. The waiter answered him in English, with a slight nod and, "Of course, Monsieur."

I don't know the difference between a bistro and a brasserie, but anyway I had steak frites, which was always a good choice in Paris because the frites were skinny and just barely crisp. The steak can be cooked à point which means "just right." If someone wanted it almost raw inside, it was called bleu. The salad came at the end of the meal, not like at a restaurant at home where it comes as a first course to keep people busy while the rest of the food is cooked. While we waited, I ate bread and butter and watched the cars and lights of Paris outside. The Seine River was just across the street, and I could see lights on the Eiffel Tower, too.

To our surprise, Mary ordered steak tartare, which was made from the best kind of beef, chopped really fine with a sharp knife, then served raw with lemon juice, salt, and little pickled things called capers. She almost never ordered meat of any kind. Duncan and I could think of nothing to say about this. Duncan just stared at her like she was eating a chipmunk with its eyes still open, or who knows what. We just stayed quiet, which was really not like us, and ate our cooked food, which was delicious.

December 8 – A Tapestry of Paris

WE WENT TO THE EIFFEL TOWER AGAIN, and so today Chris said to write a theme about something we have done on our trip. We went back to our rooms after a breakfast of hot cocoa and croissant rolls with black currant jam. It was all delicious, especially on a cold and gray morning. Even though I had already written a little about the Eiffel Tower visit a few days before, I chose to write about it again because it was still very fresh in my mind. Here is part of what I wrote today:

On the second floor of the Eiffel Tower, which was the highest platform level, there was a wide walkway around on all four sides, so I could walk around and see in all directions. On one side the Seine River was close by, and many bicycles were being pedaled along on both sides and in both directions, with the riders in coats, long scarves, and hats because it was getting colder every day now.

I could not tell which were men and which were women because we were pretty high up, but some of them had fancier hats so they were probably women. I did not see any children so they must have been in school.

The river itself was a medium brown color and swirly because of all the rain. There were three barges stacked with coal on the other side of the river, and a man was sitting on the small tugboat, waiting, and smoking. He was still there smoking, waiting, when we left to go home for dinner.

Coming down the river from the opposite direction was a glass-topped tour boat, very wide, with seats both under the cover and out in the open. I could see a waiter walking down the middle of the deck with a cart of drinks. There were not that many people outside on top because it was almost winter.

I remember last night Mary referred to these boats as bateau mouche, which meant something like "flying boat." They didn't seem that quick to me, though. I hoped we would go on one soon on a sunny day. The last time we were on a boat was a Saturday trip to the Norfolk Broads.

From another side of the tower platform, I could see the very famous cathedral of Notre Dame on its island in the river. It had two square towers standing over three arched doorways and flying buttresses on the side like we also saw in England. Even from this far away, it was quite a sight to see those open arches of stone that seem to prop up the outside of the church. Our parents were planning to take us there at dusk the next day, just before dinner.

On the third side, the city stretched out like a carpet or tapestry with the threads of streets woven back and forth, and tufts of tree-tops and gardens in almost every square. It was starting to be winter, so the colors of plants were mostly brown and rusty looking. The buildings stood out with some creamy stone colors, and also brick, along the dark streets.

Some of the buildings were covered in cloth and men were work-ing. I was told they were washing the buildings to get rid of the black streaks from smoke and soot. From here I saw some really bright, freshly cleaned ones along with older ones covered in soot.

Over to the left side I could see the entrance for an underground Metro station. These entrance stairways were covered with a curved metal structure that looked almost like vines and flowers, and there was frosted glass for the sides and roof. I already knew this from seeing them close-up.

We had ridden on the Metro three or four times. They were much quieter than regular trains at home or in England because some of the newest cars ran on rubber tires instead of metal wheels on the metal tracks. The tires, just like those on the Citroën DS, were made by Michelin right here in France! The trains would come into the stations with only a quiet hissing sound, plus a little screech-ing of brakes.

Walking around to the fourth side I could see out to the hilltop of the artists' area called Montmartre. There was a white stone church in the middle with a smaller dome in the center and small spires on each corner. It looked like a toy model. Overhead above the church were tiny specks of large birds circling.

It was getting late so I waited at the bottom of the stairs for Chris and Duncan. Finally, they came down from climbing all the way up as far as they could go. They looked cold and Chris was rubbing his hands together and blowing on them.

I liked the time I had to myself just looking around and seeing everything going on in miniature in the city below. I could watch the people, but they could not really see me. So, I stared and kept looking as long as I wanted to.

I guess I stared at people quite a lot, and Mary had quietly said that it was rude to stare. But up here it did not matter, this far away.

Gradually, it was getting louder in the streets below, with more street traffic, horns, and sirens, and the squeal of streetcar wheels. Sometimes sparks came out where the overhead rod ran on the electric wire above the street. Drivers were not supposed to use their horns, but people forgot sometimes. It must have been really, really loud before they made that rule.

December 11 – 'Let Them Eat Cake'

CHRIS'S BROTHER PETER WAS IN PARIS for a few days because he was on his way to Africa to work in a U.S. Embassy in Leopoldville in the French Congo. The only way to fly to Africa was on airlines of European countries that had African colonies. Peter was a few years older than Chris and he spoke really good French, according to Chris.

Anyway, we took the day off from schoolwork and made a trip to the Chateau de Fontainebleau. Peter took just the three of us in his rented Citroën Deux Chevaux. This was my first ride of more than a block or two in one of these cars. It was a fine sunny day, so Peter pulled back the canvas roof and the clouds rushed by, and the cool air poured down into the back seat. I didn't mind because I had on my sweater and coat. I did not have a hat, but my hair did not blow around because, really, I didn't have much at all.

The inside of the car looked unfinished: it was just painted metal on the doors and frames that showed on the inside, with no cloth or padding. The side windows folded up halfway in the middle, to the outside with a small clip to hold them. There were no cranks. The inside of the roof had no cloth covering. And it was really loud inside. The seats were more like canvas slings, with hooks and straps to hold them to the steel seat frames.

Peter had the gas pedal pushed down to the floor as we went down a long hill on a stretch of open road, slowly creeping our speed up to 90, which is about 50 miles per hour. They hooted in the front seat, and we boys held on tight in the back seat.

Chris had been reading *A Tale of Two Cities* to us when we were in London, so we knew some details about the French Revolution. The Chateau de Fontainebleau was the country palace of the French kings, and then later, of Emperor Napoleon. It was huge

Citroen DS 19, Renault, Simca,
Citroen Deux Chevaux, Peugeot 204 on the Champs Elysees

and really ornate. Even though it was early December, a few flowers were still blooming up against the building in sunny spots, and a warm wind blowing over the fresh cut lawns smelled a lot like late summer at home.

After about half an hour inside, I had seen enough. The rooms went on and on. All the gold everything and the giant pictures of the kings that they had artists paint for them so they could admire themselves. And then there were the large mirrors so the kings and queens could admire themselves even more.

A huge dining room at least 80 feet long with carved and gilt molding on the ceiling had a table that would seat 60 people for dinner. The last king, Louis the XVI, and his queen, Marie Antoinette, lived here with all their servants and luxurious stuff and fancy parties, while the people in France did not have enough to eat.

Overall, Fontainebleau was interesting but also really gross. I was glad to see the kitchen areas, the barns, and the outside. It would be more interesting to me if they showed more of this, and less of the miles of floors with their mother-of-pearl inlays and all the rest.

Last week, we went to the Bastille, the prison where the king and queen got their heads cut off, and Chris read us the plaques about how many were killed by the guillotine starting in 1789. More than 20,000! We were told that beheading was quick and did not hurt. I was not so sure.

On the way back to Paris, we ran out of gas but luckily someone stopped to help us. Peter spoke to them in French and soon they became like old friends. The man gave Peter some gas so he could drive to a gas station. When we got there, Peter filled up the man's gas can for him and they talked a little more. We got home okay. It was fun to see Chris with his brother, telling jokes and stories from when they were kids, and also hinting at some of their pranks in college.

Peter dropped us off at our hotel, and it was turning colder again. We had dinner there, and they served chicken stew in wine over noodles that I really liked. I liked every single meal at the Hotel St. Simon. Mary said these were French family-style meals. Who would not want to be in a French family, I began to wonder.

December 15 – Little Flecks of Light

ON SATURDAY, we took a family trip by train to Chartres, where there was a famous cathedral that we just could not miss. We took a taxi from the hotel to Montparnasse Station, and the train took almost one-and-a-half hours to make the trip. The trains in France were very fast, comfortable, and so smooth!

I was sitting on the right side by the window, and I could peer out and begin to see the church from miles away across the farms and small groups of cottages. The cathedral was the biggest thing around for miles. The train stopped right in the town and we went to a café for hot chocolate in the main square, which was right in front of the cathedral.

It was a sunny day, and once we went inside the towering cathedral entry, right away the interior was really bright and colorful from the stained glass. The worn and polished stone floor glowed and sparkled red, blue, green, and gold from the windows.

Over the entryway, the round "rose" window faced west into the afternoon sun and toward the main square. It was so big it almost filled the whole space between the two towers. Even though it was not yet noon, the light poured in!

We were told that when the first tower was finished and the second one was half built, 900 years ago, a huge fire broke out. They had to almost start over. They finished the later spire and rebuilt the first one. So, they were not the same at all because, by that time, styles had changed.

The walls were held up by flying buttresses like the ones we saw at Notre Dame. Before these churches were built, buttresses were built right up against the wall to hold them up. But this new kind arched out maybe ten feet from the building so the walls could be taller and the windows much bigger. And they looked more like stone wings or spider legs than something solid.

I kept looking at the rose window after being told that it had taken almost 50 years to finish. The cathedral had been there for 1,000 years, and earlier churches had been built right here for centuries before that. I could not stop thinking about what was under the ground, besides the rocks and the bodies under the cathedral floor stones.

17th Century angel with sundial, Chartres

Then Mary reminded us that these very old buildings are recent compared to the earlier buildings underneath them dating from Roman times and even before. And we'll be going to Rome in less than two weeks, so I was even more curious.

The whole time we were there, priests and some nuns in tall white hats were walking about and talking quietly with the local people in the church. Mary explained that the clothing that the monks, nuns, and priests wore was traditional for everyone from hundreds of years ago. Their clothing was meant to make them not stand out, but customs have changed!

Even though it seemed like a museum and lots of tourists like us were looking and peering and taking pictures, it was also the everyday church for the people who were living here. I saw one very small old woman slowly get up from her knees in her pew, cross herself and go to leave the church. A nun came up to her and held her elbow and slowly walked with her toward the doors. They paused for quite a while. The woman had a black scarf over her head and a blue dress down to her ankles, and I thought maybe she had been crying.

This place was so different from the English cathedrals, and I was not exactly sure why. Maybe it seemed so much older? Brighter, more like sculpture? I think I will remember this place for my whole life, with the little flecks of colored light sparkling on the stone floor.

December 18 –Gauloises, Berets, Chocolates

YESTERDAY CHRIS TOOK US ON THE METRO TO MONTMARTRE, which is a hill area of Paris where lots of artists live and work. The walk up from the Metro to the street seemed like three stories of stairs. I think it actually was.

The square had a beautiful pure white church called Sacre Coeur or the "sacred heart." I had seen it from the Eiffel Tower and written about it in one of my themes for Chris. It stood out from the other buildings because it was pure white, and we were told it had been recently washed and cleaned. Buildings all over Paris were being cleaned, and they went from being streaky black to being dark brown, creamy tan, and even peach-colored, depending on the kind of stone or brick.

All around the square in front of the church, which was actually kind of a triangle, artists were set up with their easels and pastels, offering to draw portraits. Samples of their drawings and portraits were pinned up and clipped to other easels, and on ropes tied between the many trees in the center of the square. We finally settled on one guy who did a nice job with pastel and charcoal, and afterwards he rolled them up in brown paper to take back to our parents.

It was hard to sit still for the portrait, but the artist did not seem to mind. And he was fun for me to stare at, which was my job while I was sitting there. He was watching us closely and had a cigarette hanging from his lips. He kept adding shading and small touches until he stepped back for the third or fourth time and nodded to Chris.

I had never seen or met any people before whose whole job it was to be an artist except maybe the art teacher who came to our school at home once a week. Chris said some of the most famous artists in the whole world had lived, and still lived, right here. I kept looking at people passing by to see if one or another of them was very famous or maybe was about to be! Was it the one with the beret, the Gauloises cigarette from its blue package, the companion, the worried look, the smiling face with the girlfriend nearby, the ragged or elegant clothing? Who could tell?

We got hot chocolate at a café, and Duncan and I each had part of a chocolate pastry. There was a warm afternoon sun where we sat outside under a red umbrella that said Cinzano on it. Chris got espresso and seemed to enjoy every sip!

There were small stores that sold everything from big, finished paintings in gold frames to simple sketches, and also all kinds of paint and art supplies. There were artists buying supplies, French ladies and gentlemen looking to perhaps buy a painting or drawing, and then a few people like us.

I felt like I was inside something when we were in Montmartre, more than just a corner of a city. All the art makes it feel different. It was busy and peaceful all at the same time.

Italy

Gondoliers and Bridge of Sighs, Venice

December 21 – Saltwater Streets

WE HAD ARRIVED IN VENICE TWO DAYS BEFORE. We flew first to Milan, Italy, on an Air France Caravelle, which was a French-made airplane. It had two jet engines on the back of the plane and was REALLY quiet. Arthur told me that the plane was so well-balanced front to back that their pilots sometimes tried turning off the engines and just gliding. Yikes!

Arthur had gone on a side trip to Munich, Germany, to see his friend Hans who was also a scholar of Chinese history. Arthur came to Venice yesterday. Hans was the one who liked his English cars while he lived in the country where they made the Mercedes!

Our hotel in Venice had a long view down the street to the café tables on the sidewalk in San Marcos Plaza where St. Mark's Basilica was. Just beyond that was the long waterfront on the open harbor where the hand-powered long wooden boats using long oars called gondolas were tied up. Also, there were Vaporetto motor launches tied up waiting for passengers for longer trips in the canals and on the harbor. Vaporetto was an Italian word for a gasoline engine.

It was getting colder but still not quite time for actual Christmas activities, so it was not crowded at all.

We learned about the Doge, who was the duke who ruled Venice and its empire, and about his huge palace. We walked around the outside. He was both the church leader and the government leader of Venice when it was still an independent state or country.

Instead of a street behind the hotel, there was a canal. Venice has canals everywhere; they are just like streets but made of water. Across the canal from the room where Duncan and I slept was another line of buildings. We could see people inside cooking and also hanging out laundry from windows over the water. One building was a soft yellow color and another was faded red. Motorboats came by slowly back and forth, and also we saw two children in a small rowboat. A lady stood in an open doorway holding her baby, and then a small boat stopped at her door and a man put a cloth bag of food on the doorsill for her. She blew him a kiss as he left.

People called out and talked back and forth. We heard them laughing so they must have been telling stories or making jokes. It was just like a street, but since there was no ground or sidewalk, there were no cafés or tables. Life, including the cats, was happening in the windows and doors.

Back at the plaza, the outside of San Marcos Cathedral had very detailed decorative and multicolored stonework. It had one major dome and three smaller ones. Mary said the cathedral had Moorish influence and other design styles from farther east, more than a French style of church. She said this was because the Venetian empire included many parts of Greece and other areas around the Mediterranean Sea.

We walked through the church and the square where waves from the extra high tide yesterday had left puddles of salt water. Pigeons were everywhere and people were feeding them stale bread and laughing at the birds' silly walks and how their heads jerked back and forth. We stopped for something to drink at a café, and Mary tried to order cold milk for us because we were very thirsty. After a while the waiter nodded and then she heard the espresso machine making steam.

"Boys, I think you are getting hot milk. I should have asked for latte freddo. She explained that the Italian word for cold sounds a lot like the word for hot, which is caldo." She apologized a lot and nicely asked them to add a little chocolate to the milk, and it tasted great. She was very good at making friends, even though she could pretend to be shy, and Italian men seemed very pleased when women smiled at them, and Mary was very tall and polite.

We took a ride in a gondola to a restaurant a few "streets" away for dinner. The captain, or gondolier, stood in the back of the boat and used one long oar to both paddle and steer. The boat moved pretty quickly and there was no sound except for the small harbor waves lapping against the bow as we slipped along.

Once we got there, one specialty of the restaurant was risotto, a rice dish made with butter, cheese, and mushrooms. Really creamy and smooth. I tried some but picked out the mushrooms and gave them to Mary. You could also order it with other vegetables or shrimp. Mary loved it. She said they grew the special rice here in the lowland farms around Venice.

The trip back to the hotel in the gondola after dinner was very dark. There were a few lights on in the passing squares and side canals, but the water was calm and smooth and completely black. There was no wind at all. We stopped at San Marcos Square and went to a café. Chris had espresso coffee, which is his favorite, and our parents had brandy.

Duncan and I had bubbly water, *eau gazeuse*, as Duncan called it in French, and he knew how to ask the waiter for it. He liked to say it with an exaggerated French accent and Arthur thought it was hilarious. Duncan did not often make jokes, but when he thought something was funny, he laughed like crazy. If Arthur had indigestion, Duncan would whisper to me, "Monsieur le gazeuse," and then laugh even more. It was peaceful on the plaza in the evening with a light wind bringing in the salty smells of the sea.

Looking ahead to the next day, Arthur had planned for us to go by boat to an island farther out toward the ocean where artists made glass. I think it was called Murano. Arthur hoped to buy a lamp to hang over our breakfast table back home.

I liked our stop in Venice and also was getting used to being in Italy. Everyone was very nice to children, and they seemed to think more things were funny, which was good for Duncan and me.

December 25 – Christmas Morning

We stayed at the Hotel de la Ville, 69 Via Sistina, in Rome. It had basically the same name as the small hotel in Beaune, but this one was much fancier and they speak Italian!

We opened some small presents in the early morning in our parents' room. We have always had to wake them up on Christmas as they like to sleep in. The ceilings in the bedrooms were very tall, with the molding painted a little darker color than the walls. There was a molding on the wall to hang pictures from, and the paint color changed from the wall grayish light green to almost white for the wall above and for the ceiling. The thick heavy windows pushed out to open with big brass handles to latch, and no screens. There were no window screens in Europe, at least so far.

Street musicians, Rome

We all went downstairs to the main dining room and had a delicious breakfast of flaky pastries, jam, fruit, thin-sliced salami and other meats, the special Italian cheese called provolone, and hot chocolate. There were also crispy pastries filled with sweet and creamy cheese. Italians especially liked sweet and salty things and so do I.

The hotel was near the top of the Spanish Steps and there was a fountain at the bottom, which I could hear from the top of the steps unless there was a lot of traffic noise.

Later in the morning we took a taxi to the Villa Medici for the view, which wasn't that good because it was raining. We also looked at the design and layout of the park with its many little triumphs of ingenuity and design. There were many, many fountains fed by a man-made stream and pipes. We walked along the tree-shaded walks, around the horse-riding rings and out over hills covered with grass.

Men were selling brightly colored balloons and postcards even though it was raining. It was Christmas Day and we were just about the only tourists there! We did buy some postcards because my film was only black-and-white, and Duncan and I wanted some color pictures for our collection. We were planning to have our own museum when we got home, with all the things we collected.

At Café de Paris in Little America, we had lunch of croque monsieur, grilled ham and Swiss cheese, a favorite of ours ever since visiting Paris. We took a taxi back to the hotel for a nap. Why was there a Café de Paris, named for a city in France, in a neighborhood called Little America, in Rome, Italy, I wondered?

It was still raining off and on all afternoon.

December 26 – Saint Peter's Pops Out!

WE WENT TO VATICAN CITY and St. Peter's Cathedral on the day after Christmas. The facade of St. Peter's was not as religious as I had thought it would be. It looked more like the Palais de Justice in Paris than the religious center for Catholics around the world. Still, there were some signs of religion like in the figures in stone under the upper roof overhang, and in the cross on the top of the column in the Piazza in front.

We were told that the architect meant St. Peter's to suddenly appear out of the side streets where the ordinary people lived, and not to be like the Etoile in Paris, so huge and out in the open.

During World War II in Mussolini's time, a vista, a straight road many yards wide, was built to make St. Peter's able to be seen from a long distance away. Some people said it was nice, but I thought it was ugly and spoiled the effect of St. Peter's suddenly rising up out of the small side streets of the local neighborhood. I liked the feeling of the big, beautiful building appearing almost out of nowhere from the middle of regular life.

The inside of St. Peter's was much more magnificent than anything on the outside, even though they were difficult to compare because, of course, I could not see them at the same time! The inside really took my breath away. The ceiling, colored with a gilt as rich in color as real gold—and maybe it was real gold—showed many years of careful work in the detail of the layers and coffers. Light poured in from high windows all the way around the dome, even on darker winter days like today.

The floors were marble in almost all colors of the rainbow, shaded differently with different proportions for the mosaics and patterns. Even each side chapel had its own private effect in color and also its own feeling of sacredness. Visitors were pausing to light candles and to pray quietly to the saints in these chapels. I watched their lips move and tremble even though I was trying not to stare...

We had a late lunch at a little restaurant with good pasta, lots of good tomato sauce and fresh-grated cheese. First, we tried sitting outside, but even though it was pretty warm, it was too windy, and Mary was cold. So, we sat inside by the big sunny windows in front.

Then we walked more around the square where there were lots of other Vatican buildings and offices. I tried to imagine how, inside those heavy doors, studious lawyers and priests were reading through heavy texts and writing sermons and edicts and preparing documents for the Pope to sign. Chris was fascinated, too, because his family was Catholic, and I was pretty sure he would be writing many postcards home about today's visit.

We also walked down several side streets until I started to get tired. I tried not to whine, but I may have muttered a little. Luckily, Chris did not say anything or start pretending to carry a piano over his head like he did in London. I still didn't think that was funny. I was the youngest in our family, not even eleven years old yet.

Away from the square, the buildings quickly became more ordinary. We could hear people talking and listening to music on the radio. The smell of foods with herbs and spices and tomatoes cooking for dinner drifted out their open windows. Everywhere we went, we could smell good food.

When we had walked around London, the older buildings were about 300 years old. Here, the older buildings were about 1,000 or 2,000 years old, and they were sometimes just sitting there in between the newer ones that were maybe just 800 years old. And what was left of the very oldest buildings, the ones not here anymore, were actually right under our feet, underground.

We went back to the hotel for a nap after walking up the Spanish Steps again. It was good to get back to the quiet and to sleep.

Like our parents' room, Duncan's and my room had a huge high ceiling, gold ornamented moldings around the lights at the ceiling and different shades of white for the wall panels and the surrounding moldings. It looked more like a museum or the ambassador's dining room in London than a hotel.

We had dinner at Ristorante Ranieri, a small restaurant on a main street close to our hotel. It was started by the former head chef for Queen Victoria of England. Arthur liked his Italian food and his Italian wine with it. Veal scallopini, which was sliced very thin, was a favorite, and he also sometimes liked weird things like sweetbreads. For many years Romans have liked their special foods made from the guts of animals, so there was plenty of that on the menus here. It dates back to the days of the Roman empire, I was told.

Arthur had swept-back, jet-black hair and darkish skin, so the Italian ladies thought he was one of them, I think. They glanced at him when he was on his way to the bar or the toilet. As for Mary, because she was very tall, she was always treated with respect and a slight bow from the men, who were mostly shorter. She did not seem to mind at all and always a slight smile would come to her face. Even so, she was a little shy at times. At least she told me that once.

December 27 – A Golden Fork and Spoon

WE TOOK AN AMERICAN EXPRESS TOUR BUS (we didn't do this very often) to the emperor Hadrian's Villa and the Villa d'Este outside of Rome I thought that ruins were buildings crumbled into pieces until I saw Hadrian's Villa. This was NOT a pile of rubble at all. Most of it had been excavated, and many cloisters, colonnades, and passages had been restored with the original columns, vaults, and mosaics. We had a good guide who knew all about Hadrian, the Villa, and also other later emperors. I got a good book on it and a folio of color postcards. Then, we got back on the bus and went to Villa d' Este.

My favorite Villa d'Este fountain

The Villa d' Este in Tivoli was an 11th- or 12th-century monastery changed by Cardinal Ipolito d' Este into an unfortified castle for his private use in the 1600s. There were 500 fountains run by water from springs in the nearby Sabine Hills. I had been learning that the Romans were expert at bringing water from the mountains to their cities in aqueducts.

The gardens went on for acres and acres. Even though it was wintertime in Italy, there were still a few flowers blooming in some of the gardens. I took lots of pictures, and we also bought a book about it.

Everywhere we went around Rome, there were ancient buildings and ruins. People were just going about their usual activities even though a 2,000-year-old priceless monument was crumbling right next to them!

Dinner was planned for Alfredo's, famous for its fettucine noodles, and I was excited to go. I always look forward to dinner because, as Mary likes to say, "Jonny is a growing boy." Duncan is a growing boy, too, but he is more grown up already.

The head waiter or maître d' was the one with no beard and wearing a tuxedo. He seated us at a big round table. Our own waiter came over wearing a cream-colored jacket, white shirt, and black tie. He bowed ever so slightly. His jacket was the same creamy color as the over-cloth on the table, while the underneath tablecloth and napkins were white.

The ceilings were high and carved and the tall glass windows to the street were partially covered with long white draperies. The wall electric lights were like candles with tiny bulbs. It was very simple but fancy at the same time, so clean-looking and uncluttered.

The salads were good, he promised, and I ordered one with tomatoes and dark green crunchy lettuce, a treat for mid-winter. I peeked and saw one being carried past us by another waiter. It would be served after the pasta and the main course. Our parents had dry martinis, always a puzzle to the Italians and everyone else it seemed, except the British, and then they had red wine with dinner.

I had the noodles to start, which was the official second course. The wide egg noodles were prepared for each person separately and served at table-side by Alfredo himself. He was a very distinguished man with a big smile who liked children or at least my brother and me. He wheeled over his linen-draped brass cart with its lower shelf full of bowls of cheese, butter, and olive oil.

The waiter then brought a bowl of fresh steaming noodles, which Alfredo mixed over his little burner with his special sauce of oil, butter, and cheese. Just the right amount of each, which only he knew! He lifted the noodles a few at a time, high above his special bowl so we could see how smooth and shiny they were with the butter and cheese. He put the white bowl with golden spoon and fork and creamy sauce almost the color of the tablecloth and jackets, down right in front of me to eat!

Alfredo's own golden fork and spoon had been given to him by Douglas Fairbanks and Mary Pickford. He let me eat with them. I ate out of one of his own bowls, in which he made all the noodles. Mary said that my eyes were as big as saucers!

After that I also had a veal steak with roasted potatoes and rosemary. And Duncan did, too! Boy, it was sure yummy. Then came the salad with their special dressing that was not too salty, not too tangy, and not at all sweet.

By then, I only had room for a tiny tortoni, which is creamy ice cream with bits of nuts on it, served in a little paper cup. Chris had a filled pastry called a cannoli. I was pretty sure it had some sort of sweet cheese with chocolate chips inside, like the breakfast ones, only bigger. He was all smiles with his tiny espresso coffee to go along with the dessert. And don't forget the two sugar cubes and the lemon peel.

December 28 – The All-Concrete Pantheon

My POINTY TEETH on the sides of my mouth had been bothering me a lot but just would not fall out. I had big teeth, even the baby ones, and lots of them. So this morning, I had four teeth pulled out by an Egyptian dentist. He was very nice to me and wore a green mask. His arms were the size of my legs or even larger. He had pliers that you could use to fix an engine. Arthur said he had to be strong to pull teeth which did not help how I was feeling at all. But I had Novocain and out they came. The dentist packed cottony gauze in there to stop the bleeding.

After that, we went to the Pantheon, and I was amazed by the structure. They told us the walls were almost 20 feet thick at the bottom and supported a five-foot-thick dome with a hole in the middle at the top. Our guide said it was the world's first all-concrete building. Inside there were square-stepped recesses in the ceiling dome, getting smaller all the way to the opening, so that there were the same number of these in each circle, from the ground up to the ceiling. Or so it seemed to me.

It made the ceiling seem extremely far away, disappearing into the small round opening to the sky. The opening had no glass or anything, and was called the oculus, the Latin word for eye.

They told us it worked like a chimney, letting warm air out in hot weather. Birds could fly through it, too.

Our guide said the shapes cut into the rounded surface helped with the sound and also reduced the weight. It was true that we could talk in regular voices and be heard. The lower recesses were large enough to stand up in and had statues in them. The Pantheon was built at a time when Rome had many gods, so they needed lots of those niches. After Rome became Christian, the niches got filled with statues of the saints.

All concrete Pantheon, 2000 years old!

There was a front porch supported by marble and granite columns and pillars. Behind these were double solid-bronze doors almost one foot thick and at least ten feet tall.

We went to the Castel San Angelo. It was close to the Vatican. We had seen so much, and it was very complicated. I can't describe it very well, so I better not try right now. It will be better to try another day.

December 29 – The Crossroads of History

As we walked down the Spanish Steps to get a taxi, cars were stopped in morning rush-hour traffic. Nothing was moving. A man was sitting in his car, reading his morning newspaper propped on the steering wheel and shaving with a battery shaver. I could see all this while looking down from the steps through his sunroof. I could even see the name of the paper and Mary gave me the full name: Il Messaggero.

All quiet in the Forum

We walked a little way away from the Steps to where the traffic was not stopped and got a taxi to the Sistine Chapel. There were long lines of people waiting even though it had just opened for the day; it took about 15 minutes to get into the chapel. Usually, we never had to wait in line anywhere.

We saw "The Last Judgment" by Michelangelo. The chapel was so full of famous things that it was hard to appreciate them all. It tells a really big story. Michelangelo painted the ceiling lying on his back, way up in the air on wooden platforms. His arms must have gotten so tired, and his neck, too! It took months and months, probably even with his students helping. They told us the paint was made with egg and brushed onto the cement stucco while it was still wet.

When I looked up, it seemed like there were beams and panels separating the different painted scenes from the Bible, with sky open in between. Actually, those moldings were just painted on, too. The ceiling was really a curved vault. How could Michelangelo see that from so close up and paint the curves to look so realistic from far below, down where we were on the chapel floor?

There really was too much to look at, so I looked at one section at a time. In the chapel, every panel and door was something unique and famous, but I especially liked the patches of sky and how they were painted on the ceiling. It was as if we could see through the painting and the roof to the outside above the chapel and the city. Maybe that was the feeling Michelangelo wanted us to have, like an outdoor garden. I almost wanted to lie down and put my sweater under my head to keep looking up, but the guards kept us moving along.

We went to the Vatican Museum later in the morning. There were so many beautiful, unusual, and interesting things there also, and it is hard to describe them with the proper effect. Just think about it: almost 2,000 years of relics and treasures, with so many gold objects, sculptures, holy relics, and ancient books from all over the world. I had the feeling this place was the crossroads of history, culture, and beliefs.

We had lunch at a small café where the pasta was just right. In the afternoon we went to the Roman Forum. It was hard to imagine that each brick, stone panel, and column was laid by hand by Romans from 600 BC to 600 AD. That was 1,200 years of work with many improvements, modifications, and repairs. So much marble and brick from different times and rulers.

There I was, walking where Caesar had walked and sitting in the same place that Romulus had lain in his coffin before his burial in 511 BC. How to describe exactly the feeling of being so close to the lives of real people who lived right here so long ago? It was kind of like meeting family for the first time. Here most of all, so far on our trip, I had this feeling.

We walked with Mary around the different temples and ruins of the government buildings. We walked and walked. She is a walker and has much longer legs than I do!

I closed my eyes and saw the Forum on a busy day very long ago, with men striding back and forth with scrolls, poor men in rags begging and calling out, servants trying to catch up to their Senators or Noblemen, and brick layers sweating and working in the hot sun.

Maybe the Senate would be meeting soon? Maybe there were market stalls over there on the right, with bread and salami and fruit for sale, and live chickens. Maybe there were children my age playing games. Horses and soldiers might have been patrolling. All of this happened right here, on days just like today, for more than 1,000 years.

December 30 – Burial and Sanctuary

YESTERDAY I WENT BACK TO THE DENTIST AGAIN, and he gave me some medicine because my teeth were still hurting where he had pulled them out. The stitches especially hurt. I couldn't chew regular food yet, not in the usual way, but hot chocolate was okay once it cooled off a little.

Pasta tasted really good with creamy sauce and extra cheese. The cheese on top was not the powdered stuff like we get at home, but actual fresh cheese they grated over the food at the table! They had the best ravioli in the world in Rome, at least as far as I knew.

We went to the Catacombs, where there were layers and layers of tombs and living quarters, with human bones still scattered in the slots in the stone and mud. The slots looked like bunks on a ship. Along each side of the walkways, there were burial chambers, stacked six high, for the cloth-wrapped bodies that had been preserved using eucalyptus and pine and other treatments, according to our guide. It must have smelled really bad.

Bones and worship in the catacombs

It was dark, damp, and dusty in there, and after visiting so many grand buildings with high ceilings and carvings, this place was a little creepy. The guide said that at various times in Roman history the Catacombs were also used as living quarters, but I am not sure by whom. Did they sleep on the corpse shelves? How could they breathe?

I heard someone say these had been used for slaves or servants as a place to live, or to hide if they needed to escape. Someone else said these were used for prisoners or for gypsies. Mary mentioned she thought people with different religious beliefs hid there. There was a special section of the city where Jews had to live, even though they were rich.

The bones of many people were buried there, and some bits and pieces were still there on those brick and dirt shelves, just as they had been for hundreds or thousands of years. It was really spooky and scary. It was not really an exhibit like in a museum; it was just kept exactly the way it was. I liked that because it was so realistic.

We took a taxi to the EUR Government Center, which was built for a world's fair I think, but we just looked around on the outside. We tried to visit the Roman Museum, but it was closed. Arthur said that New Year's was coming and many offices and buildings closed early for the holiday.

December 31 – Fireworks and Crashing Toilets

Ostia Antiqua mosaic ca. 100 CE

NEW YEAR'S EVE. Our parents hired a car and driver after breakfast and we went to Ostia Antiqua, the old Roman seaport on the Tiber River near where it entered the Mediterranean Sea. Rome was inland and up the river, but the seaport was where all the trading happened and where the ships had been tied up. The Tiber River was only deep enough for smaller boats. It must have been a really busy place because the Roman empire went all the way around the Mediterranean Sea, and then to England, too.

There was a lot of the Old City to see, with a bar and barbershop set up just as they had been in Roman times 1,800 years ago. There were jugs for wine and jars for food, and even hair cutting tools to see. It reminded me a little of visiting Mystic Seaport at home. There was also a half-circle stone theater that could seat 4,000 people. It was huge yet voices carried perfectly from the bottom to the top!

On New Year's Eve, Rome was alive with fireworks and flashes of light. After the driver dropped us off, we walked back up the Via Sistina to the hotel and there was broken stuff all over the sidewalks. Just before we got to the hotel at about six o'clock, we found a toilet sitting in a crater that had smashed onto the sidewalk. It had been dropped from an upper floor window. The sidewalk brick was crumbled and pieces of sidewalk and toilet were scattered all around.

People walked at the edge of the street to avoid being hit by stuff being thrown out windows. The Spanish steps were empty by that time even though it was not very late. According to the hotel desk person, the custom on the eve of a new year was to throw objects no longer wanted out into the street below. He explained this to us as if it were the most obvious thing to do, like feeding the cat!

We had dinner at the hotel. I liked having dinner "in" because it was quiet, and it felt more like home. I had roasted chicken with pasta and sauce on the side. Then we went up to brush our teeth and go to sleep. Our parents sometimes sat up for a while on this night, to drink a "nightcap," as they called it.

We heard and saw fireworks continuing past midnight along with the bright flashes of their light and colors.

January 1 – New Year's on the Appian Way

New Year's Day! I liked this day more than New Year's Eve because it was not so noisy and nobody was throwing stuff out of windows. A whole new year was just beginning. Soon it would be my birthday! Almost everything was closed for the day.

We took a taxi to the Appian Way, one of the oldest roads in Rome, from the days of the empire, and explored the area with its many early Roman tombs. The tombs themselves were sometimes simple like stones laid on the ground similar to a church floor. Some were like miniature temples with marble columns and carvings.

We had a picnic basket packed by the hotel kitchen because it promised to be a sunny day. It was really warm outside even though it was now January. In the basket there was also Chianti red wine for the grown-ups with the bottle wrapped in straw.

It was hazy and warm, almost hot by mid-morning. The trees were bare but the grass was green, and we walked on the cobblestones of the Appian Way. It stretched out a long way into the distance. We were told that this road was three-feet thick, made of many layers of rocks by slaves, including big blocks of lava that came from volcanoes. Arthur explained that this kind of road was expensive to build, but would last thousands of years, while at home the roads were only about one foot thick and needed to be replaced pretty often.

Under my feet were the same smooth worn stones walked on by cooks, slaves, and senators, and rolled on both by simple carts and grand chariots. Right there under my crepe-soled shoes! Only police cars can drive on it now. Otherwise, the Appian Way was only for walkers and maybe people on bicycles. It was a place for remembering centuries of carts and wagons.

Evenly spaced trees lined both sides, making it feel formal. We were not really going anywhere in particular, just walking around enjoying the warm hazy sunshine until it was time for the picnic. Mary called and waved to us from far down the Appian Way so that we knew it was time for the picnic! It was all set out on a café tablecloth on the grass, including red and white napkins, salt and pepper, a box of butter for the bread, and silverware.

Duncan and I really liked the salami, and Italian salami was the very best. Also, fresh crunchy bread that we could tear off in chunks, and soft cheese. Arthur liked Bel Paese cheese the best and it was extra creamy as it warmed up, almost too soft to cut. You had to kind of scoop it up. They enjoyed their red wine with Chris, and Duncan and I had fizzy bottled water, *eau gazeuse*, as he liked to call it, still cold, in green bottles.

Then we took a taxi back to the hotel, walked up the Spanish Steps, and had some rest before dinner at Tre Scalini in the Piazza Navona. This was a smaller restaurant on the lower level, a few steps down from the street. They also had outside tables under awnings for lunch in warmer weather. We had been there a few times already. It was almost always crowded, as it was on this night.

The five of us sat at a round table with a white tablecloth and dark blue napkins. Arthur ordered Vitello Tonnato, which was very thin veal wrapped around tuna, prepared with cheese and spinach, and then cooked and covered in a brown sauce. He loved it! Chris had it and he loved it, too. Mary ordered a shrimp dish with rice, and Duncan and I had cheese ravioli with a fresh tomato sauce and parmesan cheese that the waiter grated right onto our plates. He kept going and the mound got taller, and I hated telling him to stop. Lots of good bread, too! Tortoni ice cream for dessert, which was very creamy and had crushed nuts on top.

January 2 – Naked Statues and Bathing Babies

WE WENT TO THE BATHS OF DIOCLETIAN, built in about 300 AD by Emperor Diocletian. They were public baths for washing, and also for relaxing and being with friends. Groups of men and women bathed separately most of the time. But I also heard a guide explaining to another group that parts of the baths were used by men and women together for big private parties with lots of food and wine. Is that why there are so many statues of naked people here?

The Baths had been partly rebuilt so you could get an idea of what they were like before they fell to ruins, but no roofs remained. A few vaulted areas made of brick were amazing to see, with the curves intersecting at the top. The brick work overhead tapered up from the four corners of the vault. Originally it was plastered, but seeing the bare brick now showed how it had been made so carefully by hand.

The baths went on and on, room after room. There was a long trough for the men to go pee, and another open stone tray, which I thought was for washing hands. There was also a vomitorium for the men if they drank and ate too much—really gross! There were statues of reclining and relaxing naked people, beautiful columns, and large marble slabs on the floor.

We had another really nice picnic on Capitoline Hill, after walking over there, because it was another warm day. More good salami and other meats with cheese, tomatoes, and bread with butter. Afterward, Duncan and Mary went to see more of the Forum. We had already been once before, but Duncan and Mary were even more what she called "history buffs" than I was. Hard to believe. It was decided that Arthur and I would visit antique stores. I have always liked to tag along with Arthur when he goes exploring.

Duncan with Corinthian capital at the Capitoline

This whole trip, he has been going to lots of antique stores looking for treasures. He told me that to be welcomed into the store, you have to be looking for something specific, to show interest. This had been true so far in London, Amsterdam, and Paris, but not in Venice because we did not have enough time to visit any antique stores.

He was looking for a pair of torchères. He had explained to me that torchères were floor stands for very large candles and were used in formal dining rooms. At our last store visit of the day, the lady brought out a pair of torchères for him to look at. They were really ugly. He looked toward her kindly but said they were too rustic or just not right for his home.

I understood then that Arthur really did not really want these giant candlesticks at all, and they were unlikely to be found in the stores anyway because no one had used anything like that for a hundred years. It was just that he had to have a story to get the chatting started. If you went looking for something they didn't have because it was very unusual, then you would not have to buy anything, and also, maybe the shop owner would admire your taste!

He thanked the lady and she carried the heavy things back behind the curtain. Then he noticed some gold-finished wall plaques that held candles, propped up against the wall behind a wooden table. He stopped and cocked his head and picked one up.

I couldn't believe he was interested in these, as the candle holder cups themselves were being held up by naked smiling babies with wings, all painted gold. He had very good taste I have been told. He asked me if I liked them and if Mary would like them. How should I know? But I said they were nice and maybe they would be okay.

By the time we left the store he had bought them, and they were to be sent home on a ship. No torchères, but anyway these did have candles. I think we visited five or six antique stores in one afternoon. No Roman antiques though. And we got back to the hotel earlier than Duncan and Mary did. Just a few minutes, but long enough to sit in the lobby and have tea and hot chocolate. A waiter brought some very small pieces of cake with lemon filling and a sliced strawberry on top. There were just right for teatime, Italian style!

From the comfy big green chairs, we could watch people coming and going. I could stare at people without being seen and also talk to Arthur about the different people, what they were wearing and their tiny dogs. He also liked to "survey the scene," as he called it.

January 3 and 4 – **Pleasantly Kidnapped**

I ONLY GOT AROUND TO WRITING about this after we got to Athens. We had gotten up early at our hotel in Rome, packed and had a final breakfast, and one last long look down the Spanish Steps. When we got to the airport in the taxis, ready to leave for Athens, it was very crowded. Lots of shouting, waving, and traffic whistles! The taxis dropped us at the Olympic Airways section, which was the Greek airline, and we went inside.

We always needed help with the luggage because there were seven pieces. Arthur always seemed to have the right bills handy to tip the porters. The Italian lire was our fourth different money on this trip, so far, after the pound, the guilder, and the new franc! I had kept some coins from each country for my museum at home.

Arthur was informed inside that there would be a slight delay, but that we should make ourselves comfortable. The benches were hard with straight up backs, our parents and lots of other people were smoking, and there was nothing to eat or drink. And lots of shouting. What sort of comfortable was that, I wondered.

Pretty soon after that, someone came to say that it would be a little longer wait. About 15 minutes later, a man who turned out to be a bus driver with a special uniform, asked all the passengers to come with him, as we were going on a brief sightseeing trip to help pass the time.

Arthur asked some questions which brought faint smiles, kindly remarks, and comments like "Yes, of course sir," but no answers about our upcoming adventure, I guess.

As we boarded the bus, with an airline guy there now, too, Arthur looked up and said over his shoulder to me: "Well, Jonny, all our suitcases are piled on the roof of the bus, so maybe it's not such a short trip after all." There wasn't much tour information as the bus rode down the highway with the tour director pointing out a few far-away landmarks such as a church steeple here or there. There usually was not any old or interesting stuff near airports anyway.

The driver took an exit marked "Lido." We stopped at a very modern hotel and were shooed into the hotel, in a nice way, of course. People in Italy are polite and welcoming.

We got a quick and efficient welcome—room keys for fourth floor connecting rooms plus one more for Chris, and a notice for dinner at seven in the evening. Porters in dark blue uniforms disappeared with luggage into the elevators. Just like that, a whole busload of passengers was swallowed up into an empty hotel. It was a summer resort in January!

We were the first ones down for dinner, and when we entered the dining room, the band started playing some jazz show tunes that Duncan and I did not know at all. Chris was tapping one foot. There was no one else in the hotel or in the dining room except when our fellow Athens passengers gradually trickled in. It was clear that we weren't going anywhere anytime soon. Many of the other passengers were murmuring politely in what Mary identified as Greek. Maybe this was kind of usual for them.

Plates of celery and olives in melting ice were on the table, with lots of white linen and shiny silver. Where was the bread and butter, we wondered? In Italy there was always bread right away!

Duncan and I wanted to go outside because we could see that the hotel was just across the street from the beach, the famous Lido. But it was too cold, we were told, blowing sand, and soon it would be dark. Oh well.

The waiter came up to our table and spoke to the grown-ups. There was to be soup first. "You will have chicken!" he then announced. Arthur said, "But my wife does not eat chicken." Growing up she had a pet chicken that ended up being served by the cook for dinner one night, and that was the end of chicken for her forever. "Yes, of course, sir, by all means, yes. You will have chicken."

This was the part where their English language suddenly got very rusty. They seemed to agree to bring fish or shrimp, but when the plates came out, everyone had chicken. Arthur slightly raised his voice and asked to speak to the manager who came over. Arthur was always well dressed for dinner and, as I have said, had blue eyes, warm-colored skin and jet-black hair combed back on his head. We were in Italy and so, for now, he looked Italian. Soon we will be in Greece and maybe there he will look Greek?

He could also do a pretty good English accent, which worked well here, there, and pretty much everywhere!

Some pasta was brought out for Mary. She said the mushroom and tomato sauce was delicious and delicate, so she got to have dinner after all. They ordered some wine, which Mary liked to say "took the edge off." Then, after the chicken, we were brought salads and spumoni.

I kept asking and wondering whether we had been kidnapped. Mary finally paused and said, "Well, yes, Jonny, but in a nice way!" Arthur explained that Olympic Airlines was the national airline of Greece, and it was mostly government owned. The planes had to be full before they were allowed to take off, no matter what. Even if it cost them hotels and food for all the passengers! Otherwise, we would have changed to Alitalia or Pan Am, and that would not have looked good at all in their government meetings back in Athens.

The next morning after breakfast, the hotel staff were all dressed up in dark blue again, bowing slightly as we left. We all piled into the bus where the driver counted us three or four times, and off we went to the airport and to Greece. Just a day late. Arthur muttered something about how they must have "scared up" an airplane some-where, which did not seem reassuring to me at all. But it was a fine sunny day, so good for flying.

Greece

January 7 – The Blessing of the Fleet

Blessing of the fleet, Hydra

YESTERDAY WE TOOK A TRIP BY FERRY to the island of Hydra, south of Piraeus, which was the port city of Athens along the coast of the Peloponnese. The day was bright and sunny with a crisp wind off the water, a little like mid-October at home. The ferry had lots of passengers and was going to make stops at other islands along the way.

I heard the captain's announcements, but he was speaking in Greek, and the lettering was also completely different on the sign posting the upcoming stops. So I just looked and watched, took a few pictures, and tried not to get caught while I stared at people. There is just so much to see and learn by looking at people carefully for a long time, and turning away just in time to not get caught spying!

Approaching Hydra, the harbor and pier were crammed with fishing boats, from seagoing small ships to small rowing boats and sailing fishing boats, all tied up together. There was no beach and hardly much harbor at all—just piles of smooth stones where light surf broke, and the long stone pier with wooden docks on pilings.

Once off the ship, Duncan and I walked down to the water and put our hands in and it was really cold!

Duncan, Mary, Jonny at the ferry's docking controls

We walked up a narrow street only wide enough for a donkey cart, through the town and past some shops selling bread, coffee, and fruit. There were baskets of apples, pears, and grapes, mostly. And a big basket of just-ripe tomatoes. The bakery windows were open, and we saw inside where the fresh loaves were stacked up taller than the baker's head. An old woman in a white apron with white hair was using a long wooden paddle to get more bread out of the oven. It smelled SO good!!

Everywhere there were perfectly whitewashed stone houses, and a few hardy flowers here and there in window boxes. The taverns were already open, with men enjoying coffee or wine at the bars.

We walked up to an open rock ledge with railings where we could see out over the town and for miles out to sea. There was an old cannon there, too. The Aegean Sea was so blue it was almost too blue to be real water. Farther offshore there were scattered whitecaps on the water, out where the wind was stronger. There were white buildings and white clouds, too, along with blue water and blue sky.

I was trying to learn to whistle, and Duncan was trying to learn to snap his fingers, so that is what we did while we walked up and then back down that steep hillside. Me blowing and blowing and spitting, and the dull thudding of Duncan's fingers.

We had lunch in a café on the waterfront with bread, cheese, and Greek salami, and Mary and Chris had small bowls of fish soup which they said was delicious. By the time we finished, a crowd had gathered on the wharf, milling around, so we went out to the dock. A tall priest in black robes and a square black hat was speaking slowly, which began as a speech and welcome with nodding heads and smiles and then became a very long prayer. I could tell by the bowed heads and the tone of his voice when it turned into a prayer. Many people crossed themselves and most wore silver or wooden crosses around their necks.

Mary leaned over and said, "This is the blessing of the fleet," which was a centuries-old tradition in the Greek Islands at about New Year's time. The families would remember all those who had been lost at sea while fishing or on long voyages, while celebrating a new season and year.

I don't remember any singing, just the chanting and the prayers. Afterward, all the boys, including some my age, jumped off the dock into the freezing cold water to loud cheers and applause. I am not sure how the swim fit in with the prayer part, but it was clearly part of the baptism of a new year of fishing. The children were being blessed, too, along with the boats. So, I guess we all received the blessing, and I felt that maybe this would make us a little safer, too, while we traveled.

January 8 – Hide-and-Seek in a Castle

Mary ponders ruins at Corinth

WE LEFT ATHENS PRETTY EARLY and drove with a car and driver all the way down the Peloponnese to Nafplion, an ancient port and fishing city, and, at one time, the Venetian capital for all of Greece. It was a long drive of almost six hours with stops. Mary explained that after the Greek Empire fell to the Romans, and then the Roman Empire fell to the invaders from the north, different countries ruled parts of Greece. About 700 years ago, Venice had become one of the rulers of Greece and all around the Mediterranean Sea. And after that, the Turks, I think.

Birthday castle, Naphlion

We were really packed into the car with all five of us, the driver, and luggage in the trunk.

We stopped along the way at Mycenae, which was the capital city for King Agamemnon thousands of years ago. It had only been for a few years that visitors could come here at all. Before that, just sheep and stone fences. The carved stone lion over the main front gate was very famous. The guide explained the layout of the town and where the soldiers lived, the places for the bakery, and all the activities of the capital. The city walls were made of huge blocks of rock carefully fitted together. This was not like any other building we had seen.

As we got nearer to Nafplion, we stopped again at Tiryns, another ancient Greek fortress town that was much older than Mycenae. The buildings were made of really huge blocks of limestone, all cut to fit exactly. Each weighed many tons and were put into place by crews of slaves about 1800 BC.

Once in Nafplion, we found our boatman who would take us to the island fort where we were going to be spending the night. He pushed off from the harbor beach just at dusk. Our driver was staying in the town for the night. Our small fishing boat with an outboard motor headed out of the choppy anchorage for the island in the middle of the bay where the castle stood in shadow and was outlined against the darkening sky. Cold spray splashed up from the bow of our boat where Duncan and I were sitting, as we passed out from the protection of the waterfront quays and headed to the island.

On the stone pier, on the sheltered side of the fortress, hotel staff waited for us and welcomed us, including some children dressed in traditional Greek white clothing with black, red, and green brocade collars and red aprons. The girls in the group were eyeing us shyly. They were about our age and skipped away just as we stepped off the boat.

Each of our rooms was shaped out of the fort's vaulted chambers and made of whitewashed stone with simple rustic furniture. There was a bedside table and lamp, a wooden bed, a dresser with drawers, and a window through which, though closed, the wind off the harbor whistled. I liked being right out in the open water, where we could hear the wind and waves.

Dinner was served in what must have been the main room for the cannons, where the arched gun ports, about four feet high and three feet wide, were closed up with ancient heavy rusted iron plates and bolted to the stones. Outside the water crashed against the fort and occasional waves struck the iron almost like a gong, followed by sea water seeping across the floor. I felt as if the fort was moving through the water like a ship.

All the guests were seated at one long wooden table with a red cloth down the center and white napkins at each place. Dinner was a long slow event in dim light with lots of dark red wine. The lamb had been cooked in tomatoes and herbs and was delicious and tender. The bread was very crunchy and the potatoes were cooked but not mushy, with toasted edges! Duncan and I were excused early to play and explore.

We found the innkeeper's daughters waiting just outside the doors. We played hide-and-seek among the turrets and lookout platforms for what seemed like hours, even after it got dark, while the grown-ups were still down in the cannon room having more wine and brandy. A few times while we hid, we could hear laughing and a few howls and guffaws coming from down there.

As we played outside, the cool I had felt inside the castle was replaced by the warmth of running around. Duncan and I loved to run around whenever we could. Playing together with our hosts, we were not so shy anymore and neither were they. There was starlight overhead, exactly as it was when Agamemnon ruled here, and the wind calmed down to a very slight breeze.

As it got calmer and quieter, we could hear the girls giggling in their hiding places, so it was easier to find them. And we could sneak up on them and surprise them, which made them squeal and smile even more. There was one girl with very long dark braids who smiled back at me even a little longer. Her dark eyes sparkled almost like stars at night.

January 9 – **The Best Birthday**

MY 11TH BIRTHDAY BREAKFAST at the castle in Nafplion was delicious. We ate outside up on the castle ramparts looking all around at the big bay. Fresh bread had been brought over from the town, and apricot jam was on the table along with creamy hot chocolate. Our parents had hot coffee with cream, not their usual tea. They were happy, too, in the bright sunshine. Arthur was wearing his favorite dark blue Bermuda shorts and English sandals. Mary was wearing one of her "drip dry" dresses and a white sweater. She had two of those dresses, one was mostly blue and white, and the other blue and green. They had what she called "cap" sleeves and a small belt of the same cloth.

Earlier in the morning when we first woke up and were still in our rooms, our parents gave me a present! It was a small blue bag and inside were model sails for my sailboat. I was given new sails for my boat named the "Possible." Larry Sobstadt, the sailmaker, had made these tiny versions, and Mary had carried them hidden in her reticule for more than four months, just for today.

The new sails were going to be ready when we got home, including a loose-footed mainsail, which meant that there were no tracks attaching the bottom of the sail to the boom—this helped make the sail more like a wing. "Possible" was a Zip class of sailboat, one that used to be made near where we lived. It liked the choppy waters of Long Island Sound.

Chris wows the absent throngs, Epidaurus

After breakfast, once the fishing boat came back out from the harbor, we returned to the beach in Nafplion. For our return drive to Athens, our driver planned to stop at Epidaurus and at Argos. He seemed to have enjoyed his overnight in Nafplion. His dark beard was freshly trimmed and he smelled a little like fresh herbs and honey.

Our first stop was the amphitheater at Epidaurus. Many ancient cities in Greece had these partial circles cut into hillsides with marble steps for outdoor plays, music, meetings, and speeches. The Romans copied this design. It is hard to imagine or explain the size of these structures, dug into the dirt, but still here and very sturdy after more than 2,500 years.

Chris stood at the bottom and pretended to be a Greek orator on some topic. I think he was reciting something from a Greek play he had memorized in school or college. He was hamming it up with gestures and waving. He was pretty good at it. He also sang a little, which he loves to do and which he had done at school and in college.

He was always doing crazy stuff like this to tease Duncan and me. Luckily, there were no other kids around. Our parents thought it was very funny, with Arthur roaring with his once-in-a-while great big laugh. They clapped and shouted "bravo" when it was over.

We were way up in the back and could clearly hear him speaking and pausing when he cleared his throat. He said something to Mary which we could not quite hear because it was a whisper. That was kind of amazing.

There was a museum of relics and special displays of ancient medical tools. In ancient times, we were told, there were many doctors here to treat sick people. There were also several temples to visit.

We stopped for lunch at a roadside taverna, where the dense smells of garlic, fresh herbs, lamb, and fresh bread greeted us as we got out of the car. The food was delicious, especially eaten outside in the shade of grape arbors and olive trees! The driver enjoyed wine over lunch.

After we started out for Argos, Arthur scolded the driver for his driving. It was scary when he pulled out to pass going up a hill where he could not see over the top, and he had the gas pedal down to the floor in this heavily loaded car. The car could not speed up. Arthur told him to pull back into the right lane right away. Mary, who hates cars and driving, luckily did not even have enough time to get her knuckles white squeezing the armrest. It was better that way. When I looked toward her, she was watching the fields out her window. She looked over at me then, and maybe she rolled her eyes a little.

This was the second time on our trip Arthur intervened with a driver, in this case shouting at him, which was out of character for him and almost as shocking as the driving itself. And this was no Daimler limousine like we had for our Sunday in the Cotswolds.

It was a quieter ride after that and I fell asleep. We stopped briefly in Argos and then started on our way back. Mary dozed, too, or so she said afterward. It was nearly dark when we drove back into Athens, almost four hours later.

January 10 – Farewell to Athens!

WE WENT TO THE ARCHEOLOGICAL MUSEUM and saw many stone statues and golden objects from 4,600 BC to 600 AD. There were so many centuries of history here in Greece! I liked the golden masks because they were so lifelike, and also the tools and coins. There were doctors' tools and instruments from 1,000 BC. Some of these were found in Epidaurus where we went this week. There were scissors and knives for surgery, and they were not even all that rusted, even after 3,000 years.

There was every kind and shape of pottery pot, jar, and vessel. Some of the large jars for carrying wine and olives on the ships came up to my shoulders!

There were items from sunken ships and they were even better preserved because of the salt water.

We were told that the doctors used herbs and potions for pain and infection. There were jars in the museum for these medicines. Arthur, who studies ancient China, said this was common throughout the ancient world, and this kind of medicine was still in use today.

Theatre of Dionysos, Athens

We went to an international café for lunch where I had pasta with meat sauce, and then we went on a walk through the Agora. This is on one of the hills of Athens and was the main market in ancient times and also a place to gather. It made me think of the Roman Forum that we visited about two weeks ago, which was also a meeting place for people and for government activity, and also for buying and selling. The Agora was the hub of the ancient Greek city.

We went back to the Parthenon for a last view and stayed longer this time. We also went to the small museum there, but most things weren't marked so I can't say much about it. I do know that when the British controlled Greece in the 1800s, they took away many of the statues. I know this because they were pointed out to us during our visit to the British Museum in London. Here, the statues were missing from their special niches in the Parthenon. The British also used the Acropolis to store ammunition, which really made me mad since they knew how important the Acropolis was to history.

I really liked the shape of the Parthenon as a building, and the feeling inside, even though it did not have a roof anymore. Greek buildings were beautiful and so many were still standing even after thousands of years of wars, fires, and earthquakes.

There were three main types of columns that we learned about: Doric, Ionic, and Corinthian. Doric are simple. The Ionic have rams horn curls at the top, and the Corinthians have unfolding leaves at the top. My favorite ones and Duncan's, too, I think, are Doric. They sometimes have "flutes," which are like grooves in the face, and usually no added base at all. They are meant to look perfectly uniform, but to trick the eye, they have a slight taper going up and also a tiny little bulge in the middle. How did the Greeks figure that out? Chris said it was thousands of years of practice and also their study of mathematics.

Family waterfront dinner, Piraeus

We had dinner at our hotel and the food was barely alright. Afterward, we walked out in the cool narrow streets with just occasional dogs and motor bikes out in the evening. Overhead the nearly full moon shone down on the white marble of the Acropolis. It looked lit up even though there were no lights except the moon. Then, time for bed. What a long day. We saw so much. I knew I would want to come back to Greece again someday.

Turkey

January 11 – **On to Istanbul**

WE FLEW TO ISTANBUL from Athens today on a Middle East Airlines Comet 4. Nothing unusual, like some kind of kidnapping, for this leg of the trip!

This was a neat-looking plane I had admired in pictures because the jet engines did not hang down under the wings like those on the Boeing 707. The engines were almost buried in the wing shape up close to the cabin. The plane was British-made, and the airline was British-owned. The airplane also had a straight up and down tail that looked a little funny on a modern jet.

Arthur explained that Britain, France, and Germany had all claimed parts of the Middle East as theirs since the Crusades. British and European knights had come with their armies in the Middle Ages to try to take back the lands where Christianity had started from the Moslem and Turkish rulers. The Arab people had been living there all along for thousands of years, way back to Egyptian times and before that even. Even though the Middle East region now had many independent countries, there was still a lot of influence from Europe and England.

We took a taxi to the Park Hotel overlooking the Bosphorus, the very narrow channel that connected the Mediterranean Sea to the Black Sea, joining Europe to Russia and to other countries in the Middle East. From our room, we could see the shipping and the coal smoke from tugboats as night came on. Lots of ships, fog horns, and then lights from bridges and ships as it got darker. All the shipping to Russia during the winter has to pass through here because their other ports were very far north and frozen in winter. All day and all night, every day, the ships never stopped, I was told.

We had dinner at the hotel because it had started to rain. When we sat down at the table, we heard some loud talking at another table of about 15 Americans. One of the women at the table was complaining in a shrill and raspy voice about the food. The waiter was trying to be patient. Mary looked a little pained and Arthur raised his left eyebrow the way he sometimes did, and he muttered something about American tourists, and then called her "Bessy Jerk," and laughed at the clever name he had invented for this creepy and annoying person.

He said Americans were pretty bad overseas, but Germans were the worst, in his opinion. The food was alright, according to our parents. My chicken with rice, not too spicy, was just right for me. Duncan and I ate lots of chicken with rice and vegetables. Seems like a tasty meal in every country so far. The smells in the dining room were different from Europe, and I liked the slight sweetness in the smells. There was Turkish or Arabic music playing softly.

January 12 – Magnificent Mosques

Bosphoros links Mediterranean and Black Seas

WE TOOK A BUS TOUR to the Blue Mosque and then on to the Santa Sofia, which included the Museum and the Mosque. We started at the Blue Mosque which had six minarets, the most minarets of any mosque except for the mosque in the holy city of Mecca (Saudi Arabia), which had seven. Our guide told us twice, so I thought he wanted to be sure we got our facts right.

The inside of the Blue Mosque was almost entirely covered with very small, deep- ocean-blue tile mosaics, with white marble and some gold. I had never seen a blue church before, and it was really beautiful. The echoes inside, under the huge blue dome with sparkles of gold, were really surprising and musical sounding. I kept looking up until I was almost dizzy.

Emperor Constantine's reservoirs under Istanbul
still in use after 2000 years!

Our guide picked up a small rock, and offered, for a tip, to throw it up and break lose a blue mosaic piece, as a souvenir. But Arthur shook his head firmly, no. He was an historian after all, especially of ancient China, and Mary was also an historian. Ancient treasures were to be honored and kept safe for all time.

Even though it was raining lightly outside, light from the windows high up in the dome reflected off the mosaics and it seemed like a bright night sky with stars. I walked around the inside of the mosque at least two complete times.

We went on to Santa Sophia, which had many mosaics of gold and silver that were very famous and unusual. It had been a church and a temple for many religions. Santa Sophia was painted a soft yellow color on the outside. This had been its color all the way back to Roman times, according to our guide. The building was really huge with a beautiful round dome with white, gold, silver, and blue detailing and was first built as a church almost 2,000 years ago.

Emperor Constantine of Rome became a Christian. This city was called Byzantium before Constantine, but as his capital of the eastern empire, it came to be called Constantinople. Then the Turkish empire renamed it again.

Santa Sophia (Hagia Sophia was its name as a mosque) was a church for 1,000 years until the coming of the Ottoman Empire when it became a mosque.

In the afternoon we went to the Grand Oriental Bazaar where there are thousands of shops and stalls selling food, small trinkets, housewares, watch bands, jewelry, small rugs, clothing, and postcards. We bought some postcards that had good color. The smells from the food stalls of roasting nuts and meats, cinnamon and other spices, were everywhere. The smells were delicious, sweet, smoky, and spicy, all at the same time. Our parents said it was not safe for us to eat from these stalls because our stomachs were not used to the food here.

Back at the hotel we had a nap and then went to dinner at Abdullah's, an inexpensive French-Turkish restaurant. The food tasted sort of familiar and sort of different. The taste was somewhere between French, Greek, and the Indian food we had tasted in London. Roasted chicken seemed more French but had different spices. I guess that was right where we were on the map, in between Europe and India, with lots of French people visiting and living here, too.

January 13 – Wasteful Riches

THIS MORNING, we had a delicious breakfast of sweet cakes made with nuts and dried fruit, hot tea with milk and honey, and fresh oranges, while sitting and looking out over the harbor and the Bosphorus. Everything looked better because the sun was beginning to come out, and a wind was blowing the coal smoke away.

After breakfast, our parents hired a car and driver to take us to the Sultan's Palace, also known as Topkapi, where the Ottoman emperors lived and governed their empire from the 1500s until the 1800s. The gardens and courtyards were beautiful as the sun came out after days of clouds and rain.

The outside of the Palace was beautiful with all kinds of tiles and intricate stonework. But the inside of the palace was filled with every kind of wastefulness in everything anyone could ever think of. For example, one of the Sultan's dinner watches, hanging from a heavy gold chain, was not just inlaid with jewels, but was actually made of whole solid jewels, front and back; each part was a solid one-piece emerald. We were told these were, at about one-and-a-half by one-and-a-half inches, some of the very largest emeralds ever found anywhere in the world, ever.

The Sultans were wallowing in jewels, gold, and jade, while nearly every other person in Turkey and their empire did not have the shelter, food, or drink they needed. Most of the palace buildings were awful and gawdy, too much of everything everywhere, sort of Renaissance and Rococo. Fontainebleau, but worse.

We also saw Emperor Justinian's underground basilica (church) and water reservoir from Roman times; it had Corinthian and Greek Doric columns and was still part of the Istanbul water supply 1,500 years later! Even though it was underground, light came in from windows in above-ground domes that made light bounce off the water in the huge pools and tanks, and back off the tiled domed ceilings, too.

We had a simple and, Arthur said, inexpensive lunch at a restaurant on the Bosphorus waterfront where the ships were going by in both directions, and there was lots of market activity, too. More horns blaring, and the rumble of the big motors of ships in the background. Everything here seemed more crowded, busy, and active than in other cities so far in our trip. Maybe that was because this had been a crossroads for so many centuries.

In the early afternoon we saw Constantine's Palace with its beautiful mosaics. These dated from the later Roman Empire and depicted battle scenes and also farm scenes of women, children, and animals. There were mosaics of shepherds in fields and mountains with their goats and sheep.

Our driver drove us along the walls of the old city (Byzantium 900 AD–1400 AD). In about 1400 AD, the Turks from Saudi Arabia broke through the walls on the northwestern land side of the city and destroyed the city almost completely.

Later, we had coffee and hot chocolate at a café named for a famous French poet who lived here ('Pierre Lotac Changois' is what it said on the plaque by the door), and then we went home to the hotel. I had a nap while the mist rolled back in over the Bosphorus. The ships passing felt restful to me and put me to sleep.

Dinner at Abdullah's for the third time. When our parents found a place they liked, we went back again and again. Most tourists just pass through once, I guess, so when we came back, we were treated to such a great welcome as if we had been old friends for years. Lots of smiles and shaking of hands. Turks were very warm and hospitable. Duncan, Chris, and I were given free dessert, which was a flaky pastry or cake with walnuts, raisins, and honey. Nothing French about that! Chris liked to have his usual espresso coffee with sugar and lemon peel, the Italian way, along with his dessert. Turkish coffee is famous around the world, and this is the city to taste it!

January 14 – A Battered Briefcase

WE PACKED UP FOR A 12:00 FLIGHT TO BEIRUT, then had hot showers and dried off with those amazing thick and fluffy white Turkish towels made from Egyptian cotton.

Once we got to the airport, we discovered that the flight did not leave until almost four in the afternoon. We spent a lot of time in airports during this part of our trip. We had snacks of rolled up sandwiches, and Chris had his last Turkish espresso.

Arthur's briefcase was packed with all the tickets and carbon copies and receipts for payments, as well as receipts for the money exchange which he says he will have to show to our government when we go home. He has all the money receipts organized in the leather file folders built into the lid of his briefcase. The briefcase was brand new for the trip, but it was not new anymore! It was worn and I thought it looked like it had traveled across a desert on the back of a camel.

The Pan American Boeing 707 arrived in Beirut by dusk. They cooked dinner for us on the airplane. As we got close to the airport, the pilot announced that it was 24 degrees in Beirut, and everyone gasped until we realized he was using Celsius temperatures. Arthur had told us that in a few years our country would be using meters and Celsius, too.

Once we were on the ground and had gotten through the airport, it seemed like a summer evening. Stars glowed in the sky and palm trees lined both sides of the main streets as we drove into the city in our usual set of two taxis.

Lebanon

January 15 – Discovering More Dickens in Beirut

WE DID ARITHMETIC AND SPELLING LESSONS in the morning, and lots of them because most of our other schoolbooks had been sent by ship from London or Paris to Tokyo. I think the trunk weighed 80 pounds! Chris assigned us to write a theme, so I wrote about visiting the Blue Mosque in Istanbul, and also why it was called Istanbul, Byzantium, and Constantinople over many years, but was still the same city. Well, almost, except for the parts that were destroyed by different conquerors each time they took over the city.

We had a tasty lunch at Quo Vadis, which I thought would become a favorite because everyone in our family, including Chris, likes Italian food. We walked to the beach in the afternoon for a good swim in the surf. The water was very clear, light blue, and cool, and almost nobody was there because the air was only 71 degrees. For the people here, it was winter.

After lunch and the beach, we had a rest in our room. Chris decided to explore and take a walk in the hotel neighborhood. Later, he was really excited to tell us about a small store he found that sold used books because he had seen a copy of Charles Dickens' *David Copperfield* in the window. He bought it so he could read it to us. It was very thick and looked like it had been read many times before. Chris said he would read some of it to us most nights before we went to sleep. I could tell he wanted to re-read this book himself. It was by the same writer as *A Tale of Two Cities*.

Our parents went to have drinks and dinner with the American ambassador. I was not sure how they knew them, but there was some event that had been arranged. They always seemed to know lots of people and to have what they called "Letters of Introduction." Mary said they tried to contact the embassy in every capital we visited just so people there would know that Americans were in town, in case something bad happened.

Chris took us to an okay Italian restaurant with good ravioli and pizza with lots of cheese. I was glad we did not have to go to the embassy. I was thinking that even bad pizza would be better than the food like we had at the embassy in London.

Chris was pretty strict but let the two of "us boys" carry on a little, which was a fun change from family dinners, which were usually at fancier restaurants. I was thinking Chris was probably missing his brothers and sister. At least Duncan and I had each other.

It seemed that Lebanese people also loved pizza, because there were people standing in line way out the door and down the sidewalk. We have not been anywhere yet where people don't like pizza.

After we got back to the hotel, Chris started reading to us from *David Copperfield*, which he called "Copperhead," and it got interesting right away. Chris told us that this was how any good book should start so you would keep on reading. It was a very long book, so we had lots of reading time ahead of us. I wondered what kind of story it was that would take more than 900 pages to tell. I guess we would find out, but probably not very soon.

January 16 –Seven Layers of Civilization in Byblos

WE DID MORE ARITHMETIC AND SPELLING LESSONS in the morning, and Arthur went to see the doctor. Maybe he will have to go to the hospital tomorrow for something about his foot.

After a quick sandwich lunch at the hotel, we went with a car and driver north of Beirut toward Syria to visit the ancient city of Byblos. Our parents explained that this city was actually one of the very oldest in the world and had been lived in for nearly 6,000 years!

The road we followed continued very near the sea, so we could see fishing boats and also surf on the beaches and rocks. Then we drove close to the harbor front in Byblos where fishing boats were tied up and anchored out on moorings protected by a stone jetty. Their triangular lateen sails and rigs lay loosely folded on the open decks. Some had outboard motors, too. Nets were drying from poles on the jetty.

On the hill behind us there was a huge fort dating back to the Crusades. But first we walked around the village and came to a place where construction digging was going on, as they were making improvements to the dock and harbor.

Duncan and I looked down into the hole, and our guide explained that if you dig deep enough you will find seven layers of different settlements here. Duncan was interested in the Phoenicians, and their layer was way down at the bottom, from 3,500 BC!

Ancient burial vessel, Byblos

Archaeologists were picking through the piles and along the trench, taking pictures and writing in their notebooks.

I only counted six layers, but some of the separation lines were a little fuzzy. The Romans were about three down from the top. Like the day before yesterday around here. The ruins of the Crusader settlement were at the top just below the modern times and just looked like regular junk.

Along the waterfront in town there were shops selling fish, bread, meats, sweets, and souvenirs. We went into one and found all these excavated items for sale, sitting crowded on dusty glass shelves. Thousands of them! Duncan picked out a small Phoenician burial pot and I chose a Roman oil lamp, because the burn smudge from the wick was still visible after being buried for 2,000 years! It had coiled circular designs on it like a snake or maybe the wick, Mary said.

We sat on the huge stones along the waterfront, and I looked out past the fort toward the harbor entrance. I kept thinking about all the people who came and went from here for all those thousands of years. Such a long time! Some of their families and descendants still lived here. It was getting late in the afternoon. I wondered if the archeologists were finding people's bones, too, in addition to broken pots and tools.

For the people doing the harbor construction, it was just another day among the broken pots and priceless bits and pieces, I thought. For me, it was a huge window full of treasures and secrets, just waiting for the right moment.

Back in Beirut, we had dinner at a Spanish restaurant. Our parents enjoyed the fish. Duncan and I had a rice dish with chicken and tomatoes, kind of like the dinners we had at the Spanish place in London. Chris had a rice dish with fish, chicken, sausage, and little, tiny clams.

I remembered those Spanish food smells from London. They were spicier and richer smelling here, where it was warm, and the smells kind of hung over the outdoor dining courtyard. I liked that because it's like having the food all over again, but through my nose, while watching the palm trees against the night sky blowing slowly back and forth.

January 17 - Relics From Long Before Rome!

ARTHUR WENT TO THE HOSPITAL to have an operation on his toe while we did lessons. Then, in the afternoon we went to the new Archaeological Museum with Mary and Chris while he rested. His foot was okay, Mary told us.

The museum had exhibits of the best objects and relics found in every one of the sites we have visited or are going to visit here in Lebanon. Some were shown with photographs of the exact location and moment of discovery; others have been repaired or restored. I liked the enlarged photographs that showed early archeologists camped out in tents in the desert around places like Baalbek. In the background sheep and goats were wandering through the temples. Actually, they seemed to be staring at the building ruins just the way I did, as if they were trying to figure things out. Or maybe it was lunchtime.

Objects from Byblos, Tyre, Sidon as well as Baalbek, and many other sites, were displayed with historical explanations. Some of the very earliest people from here were the Hittites and the Sumerians. The Sumerians did lots of astronomy and arithmetic, farther back than 3,000 years BC. There were just a few fragments and items from that time—these were the first people living in actual cities in the region, as far as historians knew.

We had dinner at the hotel, the Alcazar, on Rue Minet El Hosn. Hotel food was almost the same everywhere, but not quite. Arthur said that they had to offer food that everyone would like, at least a little. There were French, Turkish, Syrian, Japanese, and Indian businessmen staying at the hotel, so that is a lot of different people to make food for.

January 18 - Sidon and the Israeli Frontier

WE WOKE UP EARLY TO HAVE BREAKFAST, including French-style croissants with butter and plum jam. Then we went to meet our car and driver under the hotel entry roof, as we had done several times before. We were headed to Chateau de Beaufort, a Crusader castle in the south, close to the Israeli border.

Once we got close to the castle area, there were soldiers everywhere on both sides of the barbed-wire fence. Two soldiers accompanied us to the castle because it was in the military zone. There were guns and cannons at the castle that the Lebanon army had put there, pointed toward Israel. This was not part of an exhibit. But there were also rusty old cannons on display that were at least 400 years old.

The castle was located high on a rock mountaintop, overlooking the plains below, with a view far into Israel. I did not understand what the war was about.

From there we went to lunch in Sidon on the coast, where our driver found a simple restaurant near the harbor with excellent sandwiches rolled up in thin flatbread. They had a creamy bean paste here with lemon in it that they spread on sandwiches.

After that we visited another Crusader castle like the one in Beaufort but better preserved. Different guides had different ways of describing the Crusades, why the knights came, and what happened. But I think each one was saying nicely that he really wished they had just stayed home. Lebanese are kind and hospitable, so they would not say anything really bad. But the Crusades were a big part of their history, even now.

Then we went to Beiteddine Palace from the 18th century, tucked away up in the hills, with beautiful stones and mosaics. It was built as a hermitage for Moslem philosophers and then converted into a palace. That was a big change.

After that we went back to Beirut for dinner at Quo Vadis with Chris and Arthur. Mary went to dinner with the American ambassador. Our parents had visited the ambassador and his family three times so far during this visit. I wondered what they were talking about.

Beiteddine Palace

January 20 - **Pondering Ruins**

WE HAD ANOTHER GOOD DINNER last night at our parents' favorite restaurant, Quo Vadis. Chris told us this means "whither goest thou" in Latin, which he had studied in school for years. Arthur had something with a creamy mushroom sauce, and Mary, who never ate chicken and mostly hated beef, had a noodle dish. She liked fish, though. Chris ate everything including the parsley. Duncan and I had chicken with lemon and rice.

Our parents hired a car along with a driver named Maroon to go to the ruins at Baalbek on the road out of Beirut to the east. After slowly finding our way through the narrow streets of the older part of the city, we got to the main roads. Leaving the city and heading out into the dusty desert, on the right side were rubble buildings with scrap rusted-tin roofs held down by large stones on top. It looked like ruins. Kids were running everywhere.

Our parents said these were Israeli refugee camps for people who used to live in Palestine before Israel became a country. I did not see any playgrounds or anything that looked like a school. Why didn't they have schools and playgrounds here like the other kids in Beirut? It was like another whole city, even a different country, of rubble and rags, inside the edge of the modern city of Beirut. Clothes were hanging up to dry in the dust. It was January but it was warm outside.

After some miles across dusty desert roads, with a mountain range visible in the distance, we came to Baalbek in the northern part of the valley that is east of Mt. Lebanon. These Roman temples were some of the largest in the world, we were told, and some of the single stones used across the top over the columns weighed more than 100 tons.

Baalbek had three main temples, all of which were erected before the stones were carved. The workers lay on their backs on planks to carve. Just like Michelangelo had to, but this was outside in the hot sun. They were using chisels in stone, not brushes and paint. We were told that all the workers were slaves.

There was a large temple to Jupiter and a half-circle amphitheater that the Romans used for dances with an anteroom for preparing for the events, which was also huge. On both sides of the temple were pools used for washing the animals before they were to be sacrificed on the altar in the center. Behind the altar was a meditation space where the Romans went to pay their respects to the gods. Another temple nearby was dedicated to Bacchus, the God of wine. It was smaller but just as grand in style as the Jupiter temple.

How did they get those 100-ton stones up there on top of the columns? Even though to some visitors they were just ruins, I really liked these places where people lived so long ago, had their special ceremonies, and were now empty. I liked guessing about the people and asking questions. Where was their water, their food, where were their bathrooms?

We had lunch at a summer resort town at the base of Mount Lebanon, passing the turn-off for the road to Damascus. We walked part way up and saw some small piles of snow!

I kept asking if and when we were going to go to Damascus because it had been on our list of cities, but apparently that part of the trip had been cancelled. Already we had not stopped in Teheran

Roman temple ruins, Baalbek

and Isfahan in Persia. Our trip did not include Egypt, and I had been really hoping to see the pyramids. Arthur said it was getting more difficult to travel in many countries in the region, and that was not difficult for me to imagine.

I had read something about the hanging gardens of Babylon and the Fertile Crescent, but I guess those places were also hard to get to. And, I think our parents were getting a little tired with all the short stops and changing hotels and money every few days.

Back in Beirut, while our parents went with friends for dinner at Espana, the favored Spanish restaurant, Duncan and I asked to go with Chris to Uncle Sam's for hamburgers. There's a cook in there with a red, white, and blue shirt and a tall white chef's hat who looks a lot like the guy on the sign, except that this chef was Lebanese.

January 22 - Ancient Tyre

THE MORNING WAS ALREADY HOT AND DRY by the time we finished breakfast and our car and driver, Maroon, arrived at the hotel entry. The cars here were a mix of older American models and newer French cars from makers like Renault and Citroën. Everywhere there were smoky Mercedes Benz diesels used as taxis. At home, a Mercedes is a really fancy and expensive car, but these are not at all. The backs of them were all black from exhaust, so much so that I could not even see the license plates.

It kept getting hotter on our trip to Tyre. Thankfully the ruins we visited were above the waterfront and right near the harbor, and there was a nice wind blowing off the water. I could almost see the sails of ships passing by 3,000 years ago.

The Roman ruins here were well preserved and so have not been restored or rebuilt according to some modern person's own idea of what they originally looked like. There were some drawings and pictures to see on placards, but the ruins themselves were fine for me to look at just as they were. We have seen a lot of ruins on this trip so far, many from the Roman era. The arches and columns and mosaics were becoming familiar. It was almost as if I could read what was there just from the old outline of the ruins.

The columns and building designs in Tyre were pretty much the same as other Roman towns from the same period. What was different in Lebanon and in Tyre was the much older Phoenician cities and relics, which had been recently uncovered and preserved. This city already had old winding stone streets and ancient buildings thousands of years old before the Romans arrived. So hard to imagine, but it was all right there in plain sight.

We had a late lunch in the "new" town, which is only 1,000 years old, which is like last week around here, before heading back to Beirut.

January 23 - **Farewell to Fast Food**

IN THE MORNING, we went back to the Archaeological Museum to see more artifacts from the places we had just been visiting. It all made more sense here, and the best artifacts were preserved and protected. Arthur got a first look at the museum now that his foot was better.

There were pottery figures from the Hittites and ancient Assyria. In the gift shop, we bought a replica of a clay Hittite figure that looked like he was surprised while he talked on the phone. I knew they did not have phones then, of course. Arthur, who was the one most interested in ancient culture, seemed to really enjoy the bronze and gold items. He got very serious around ancient culture because he was paying close attention, thinking, and maybe comparing the objects and art to what he knew about ancient China.

We had lunch at Uncle Sam's and were told these might be our last hamburgers with French fries for quite a few months. We never visited the Kentucky Fried Chicken in Beirut, the last outpost of Europe, and that didn't bother me at all. I liked the chicken at the Spanish and Italian restaurants just fine.

They don't have Kentucky Fried Chicken where we are going in Asia, either, I was told. Not really sure what those places were doing here at all. Do Arabic people really like fried chicken?

Then we had naps and packed up to fly to India. We left the hotel late in the afternoon.

India and Nepal

January 24 - A Mixed-up Looking Building

THIS OVERNIGHT SIX-HOUR FLIGHT on the Boeing 707 was our first on Air India, but the plane was just about the same as our plane from New York to London. Air India was the big Indian international airline that flew all over the world. It was pretty quiet in the cabin after they served us chicken curry for dinner, which was good and not too spicy. After the crew served tea and cookies with coconut and honey, the captain turned the lights down.

Arthur was across the aisle from me, and every time a stewardess swished by in her long silk sari, it brushed across his face and woke him up. He was not happy.

Most of the passengers were Indian, with a few English people. As I tried to sleep, listening to the rush of the night outside, I felt how far I was from home, and getting farther by the minute. I did not know anything about India except that we would be traveling there for more than a month.

We actually landed in New Delhi first, which was the capital, got off to go through customs, and then flew on to Bombay, another two hours. It was 81 degrees and really sticky-hot when we arrived in Bombay.

We took a visitor bus from the airport that made several stops at other hotels before it arrived at the Taj Mahal Hotel in downtown Bombay. The hotel was right across from the main waterfront where ferries come and go. The big ships docked farther away where there were cranes and trucks ready to load and unload cargo.

To me the hotel sure was a mixed-up looking building. I got so confused by the Victorian bay windows, Indian-style balconies, a center dome like St. Paul's Cathedral in London, and corner domes like those of a Turkish mosque.

Our hotel had two doormen at all times, dressed in dark red uniforms with a little gold braid on the chest and shoulders. Arthur said we were going to have all our meals at the hotel, something that was called a "Full American Plan." If you get lunch on your own, that was called a "Modified American Plan," or MAP. What did the other travelers do?

Inside the lobby, with its stone, marble, dark wood, leather, and sumptuous carpets, the massive fans were moving on leather belts from motors off to the side. This made the lobby feel like a tropical version of a grand English country home. It was explained to us that India was still filled with British colonial life even though independence had happened 14 years earlier. Arthur said sometimes it might feel more like England than Asia. After all, he said, the British had ruled India for almost 200 years.

We got huge rooms looking out toward the harbor, with those big overhead fans that we used to see when visiting Mary's family in Florida and Alabama. They turned slowly overhead all day and all night, always humming. The windows at the front of our room were more like doors, and they opened onto a small balcony where we could walk out. Below, the traffic was constant, even late at night!

Mary had explained that Indian people are mostly Hindus, who do not eat beef, and some Moslems, who do not eat pork. Many Indians only eat vegetables, beans, and rice. All the food was spicy, but not too spicy when cooked and served to foreigners!

Anyway, at dinnertime we all went to the dining room, which had huge high ceilings and white tablecloths. Our parents ordered martinis and Chris had one, too. They are made with gin, which is an English favorite, and sometimes served with bubbly tonic water. Mary liked those. The roasted chicken I had was delicious, cooked in a clay oven, they told me. Dessert was a creamy sweet custard with raisins and cinnamon, and other spices, too.

January 26 - **Carved in Stone**

ON OUR FIRST MORNING, Bombay's British-style waterfront was full of Indians going to work, shopping, begging, and living on the street. The big bank buildings like Barclays stood silently in the steaming morning as white men in black cars with brown drivers in black caps arrived at their offices.

The harbor water was quite still for what promised to be a very hot day even though it was winter. We walked along the quay where small waves washed a dense mat of garbage, wood, bamboo, oil containers, dead fish, and trash back and forth along the stone wall.

Set back from the waterfront, across the busy road with its streams of bicycles and black London cabs, and out of earshot of the street vendors, were the buildings and offices of business, tourism, and finance, including our hotel.

On one street corner right across the main road was an English teahouse, where I could see staff freshening up the tables after the breakfast guests had left. The teahouse was beginning to refill with well-dressed British and European women in hats and sometimes gloves, gathering for tea. "Dreadfully hot for this time of year, don't you think?" one of them seemed to be mouthing. Another: "I do wish the boys would bring more really hot water for the tea."

Turning back toward the waterfront, I could see a small island about one or two miles away in the haze. We were heading out there today aboard a harbor ferry to visit its ancient temple. I was told by our parents that the island and temple were holy sites. Today, like every day, visitors and pilgrims would be cramming the ferry, some carrying offerings of food and flowers.

Once we were on board, I noticed the boat was leaning a lot to port against the stone pier as more and more passengers crowded aboard. People were everywhere, packed back-to-back and side-to-side in a solid sweaty mass when the mate blew his whistle. After the mooring lines were undone and thrown back on deck, the ferry pulled away, rolling slowly on the swells, and puffing black coal smoke. The deck mate was moving quickly all around the boat, barking orders to the boat boys and calling them with a loud crack of hand and finger snap I had never seen before. Not just fingers, but a snap of the right index finger across the pad of the left index finger. I asked Arthur to look and listen with me.

Jonny and Duncan on ferry to Elephanta

When we docked at Elephanta Island, walking down the two-plank-wide gangway with its loose rope handrail just on the right side, we could see the steps ahead led up to the temple opening. The building was made by carving everything out of the natural solid rock, leaving only the stone of the building and its components there for us to see. The beautifully carved but simple entry columns rose up out of the rough rock, and then, above their capitals, disappeared back into the natural rock form. It was as if the columns had been there, but unseen for all time, until artisans and priests found their beautiful forms hidden in the rough rock.

The temple ceiling was raw hammered stone as were the floors and walls, although the walls had been smoothed and painted in the distant past. Visitors examined outlines of frescos with small flashlights, tracing fragments of blue, red, and saffron-yellow drawings dulled by the centuries. Some people knelt, eyes closed and lips moving slightly, while others like us, looked around, took pictures, and tried not to look too out of place.

Small plates of fruit and nuts were lined up along the walls, and the sour, earthy smell of what Arthur said was incense drifted around the temple.

After more than an hour, the ferry's shrill steam whistle blew twice to call us for the trip back to the city. Once back on the harbor ferry for our return trip, the mate was again calling the boat boys with the sharp snap of his fingers and coiling the dock lines as the brown water curled away from the bow. I watched him and followed him as closely as I could around the ferry, hoping to get a better view of his hand snap.

Once we were back on shore in Bombay, and steadying ourselves on land again, I started practicing this hand signal. I needed harder calluses on my hands and bigger hands. It was a little like the first time eating with chopsticks. Nothing British about that!

January 28 - Into the Indian Interior

WE TOOK A LATE AFTERNOON TWO-HOUR FLIGHT from Bombay aboard an Indian Airlines DC-3, out into the flat, dry country of the south-central Indian interior. Indian Airlines flew all the smaller planes inside the country.

The DC-3s were "tail draggers" that taxi on the ground with the tail down, and steer on the ground with that little tail wheel, too. It was only when the plane was about to lift off the runway that the tail came up. I watched several DC-3s take off while we waited in the airport.

Boarding the plane, which had two seats on each side, was a climb up the aisle to our assigned seats after ducking in through the rear door. Arthur's seat row companion was a very tall Indian Army officer in khaki dress uniform, his shirt covered in medals and badges, a big mound of silver hair wrapped up in his turban, and a large, shaped and trimmed silver beard.

He was quiet during takeoff and through most of the flight, until he leaned over to Arthur as we neared the end of our flight. "Tell me, sir, do you have these aircraft in your country?" "Oh, yes indeed!" Arthur replied, and I then remembered that I had flown in one once to see my grandmother, a puddle-jumper flight from New Orleans to Mobile, Alabama, when I was about five years old. The officer seemed pleased with the answer and then continued looking out the window into the fading light.

Before long, as we approached the airfield at Aurangabad, I could make out the grass below and then a line of flaming kerosene torches on each side of the runway. Goats, cows, and sheep were scurrying off into the brush. We did not land right then, but came around again, in the blue-green twilight, once the animals had scattered.

We landed with dust coming up around the wings as the tail settled to the grass, the big tires rumbling. We stopped outside a small building with a couple of bare lightbulbs casting shadows on the mostly dark faces inside. Boys barely my size carried our luggage from the plane through the terminal shed to the roadside in front of the airport where all our bags were loaded into a taxi.

There were no sounds at all other than night insects. Then a truck horn blew far away in the night, and a few voices were talking in the airport as the plane was loaded for the return trip to Bombay. There was the sound of bare feet and sandals shuffling in the loose dirt.

Arthur hired a taxi driver with his old Hudson from the 1940s to take us to our hotel. After a few hand cranks on the front of the engine, the driver fiddled with the wires behind the dashboard for a few moments. Then, a few more cranks and the motor caught with a growl and several puffs of smoke. We chugged off, loaded down with four of us in the car and the driver's friend in another car behind us with Chris and all the luggage.

Even though this was a country of 400 million people, we were traveling through a totally windless quiet, in complete night darkness except for our car's headlights. It seemed almost uninhabited.

Arthur, especially, was excited for this part of the trip where we would be visiting the world-famous cave temples. We had just visited Elephanta in Bombay, so I was already curious, too!

The hotel was two low buildings with a covered veranda along the front. We settled into simple rooms with one lamp and an electric fan overhead. When we sat down for dinner, which was mutton and potatoes, Arthur told us about the Sikhs, a separate religious group from northwestern India, in an area called Punjab. His seat companion was from this group. Over the years, he said, many Sikhs had served in the British army and fought in the world wars. He said they were known to be calm, strong, and fierce. Since independence, they had become a much-honored part of the Indian Army.

January 29 - **Beggars and Buddhas**

A thousand years of temples carved into the cliffs

AFTER A BREAKFAST OF BUTTERED TOAST, marmalade, and tea, with cut up oranges on the side, the well-worn 1939 or 1940 (Arthur reported) Kaiser sedan our parents had hired arrived at the hotel. The driver was tall and very thin, and very dignified, too. We set out for Ajanta, the site of ancient carved-out temples in the canyon walls, and intricate wall paintings. The hotel had packed us a picnic basket of canned meats, crackers, and bananas.

Adjanta cave temple interior entirely carved into solid bedrock

Our driver asked us to please push ourselves over to the right side of the car as much as possible, as the left back springs were rusted and all broken except for one last layer, or leaf, as Arthur called it. Each bump made the car surge and weave on that springy side, and I sat in Chris's lap to push the balance even more to the right. It was a two-hour ride to Ajanta, and on the dusty roadside small children poked out of the bushes, curious about the arrival of a car. I looked through the bushes and could see behind them rows of small shacks and clothes hanging to dry.

After about an hour, I finished a banana snack and threw the peel out the window. I looked back and was really surprised to see the nearby children diving and scrapping for the treat. I was having my second food of the day and they probably had not had anything yet. I usually get hungry for a snack every few hours. I could not think of what it would be like to not eat all day. I asked Mary how many children here in India did not have enough to eat, and she said a great many. I felt very sad sitting in the car, until we got to the temples.

When we got to Ajanta, there were several other cars there already, with English and Indian tourists. Many starving holy men watched us with their hollow eyes. They stretched out their bony hands and shrunken arms for money or food. Arthur said there was nothing we could do for them. I had never seen this before, ever. I held Mary's hand and kept my head close to her shoulder.

When we got to the edge of the canyon, I could see that the caves were carved in a semi-circle of a canyon wall, completing about one quarter of a circle that followed a dry river bottom below. They were hewn out of 100-foot-high solid, smooth cliffs of rock.

The earliest cave temples were simpler and had plain columns with fewer details but still many beautiful statues and wall carvings of Buddha in meditation. These older temples had ribs of plaster added later on the plain stone columns. Additional plaster had been added, centering on the keystone above the statue of Buddha, which made the temple entrance look like it was made with stone beams like a regular building. The guide explained that these were 400 years older than the later temples, making them almost 1,300 years old!

I was pretty sure that these caves were about the age of the temple at Elephanta, but much larger and more varied. We went into at least seven temple rooms that I can remember, walking along a rock ledge way above the bottom of the river canyon. Mary and I do not like heights at all!

Each temple room must have been for a different purpose. Some seemed to be like sleeping or living rooms, others with more decorative carvings and traces of paintings.

Many of the later temples had beautiful statues of Buddha in all the possible postures and positions I could think of, and then some!

Several times we paused to look back and forth on the canyon wall at the carved-out buildings inside the massive rock. Above the carved temple entrances, the stone surface became its natural broken surface again, as it had been shaped by nature and the river over millions of years. Going inside the caves, I felt the hard work of removing all that stone, all the time, the years and years, of hammering and carrying, shaping and carving.

Some of the more massive later-era temples had paintings of Buddha thinking or making a speech, and others were illustrated with sober, thoughtful monkeys representing the Buddha, too, I was told. The carvings were all of Buddha and other holy figures thinking and dancing, as well as horses and animals being ridden, and many other animal and human figures. A lot of the paint colors and lines had worn away, but we still saw the outlines and some of the colors.

As I stood there, I felt the stillness and peace that seemed to come from the holy work of so many lifetimes here. It was very quiet, except for the shuffling of our feet, occasional bird calls overhead, and just away from the temples, outstretched beggars' hands and pleading voices and eyes. The begging for "baksheesh" was like a continuous background moan. The guides tried to shoo them away, but they kept following us. Our parents said we were not to give them money.

There were no signs or information plaques like we sometimes saw at museums. It was just us, the other visitors, the guides, and the quiet heat of the day. We were seeing the temples as they were, and had been, for centuries. A few postcard vendors followed us around, so Mary bought several packages. Our guide was very knowledgeable, and Arthur quietly explained that such a job would be a great honor, and so important for him to have steady work to support his whole family. Later I saw that Arthur tipped our guide additional money. Our parents had more information from their own studies about the history of the temples and the religions practiced here.

I learned that three different religions, Buddhist, Hindu, and Jain believers, built, used, and revered these places for almost 1,000 years. They lived, prayed, and worked here together. Even after the Moslems came, they, too, used the temples for a while for their own worship.

But overall, the Moslem conquerors were less respectful, so damage was done to the temples, and they fell into disrepair and were no longer used or properly protected starting several hundred years ago.

Later, we were told, local and other collectors and merchants broke away and stole parts of the temples and sculptures for private collections and museums, especially in England and other countries. I wondered if maybe we would see them somewhere when we returned home, maybe at a museum in New York.

The missing and broken parts bothered me quite a bit. It was not that things were missing, but that treasures had been stolen, and no one was here to protect them. It was a similar feeling as I had when looking at the empty niches at the Parthenon. But those statues at least had been taken for museum safekeeping and Greeks knew where they were, even if they were mad about it. Here, the damage from differing religions and the destruction of so many centuries of work for no reason really bothered me.

Pilgrims still sometimes stay in the temples even now as there is no other shelter anywhere else nearby. And here we were in the hot midday sun wandering about with plenty of food, a car and driver, and an airplane to take us to our next place in a few days! What I saw and felt here I think will stay in my mind forever.

On the way back to Aurangabad, we stopped at Aragbezel's tomb (he was a king in the mogul times) and took off our shoes before we entered in our socks, in order to be respectful. Within moments of our arrival at the tomb, all kinds of beggars, holy men, and Moslem believers, arrived to beg or sell some small objects or postcards. We bought some bundles of postcards so we could have a few color pictures to add to my black-and-white photographs.

We saw some monkeys scampering all over the tomb. We ate our hotel box lunch at the tomb under a big tree with monkeys watching us from above, catcalling to each other all around us. The driver had some fruit that he ate by himself.

Once back in Aurangabad at our hotel, we had a rest time and sat in the shade under the porch roof until it got dark. We had mutton and potatoes for dinner, this time a goulash stew. There were only a few lights and as darkness fell I was ready for bed anyway, and so was the whole family.

January 30 - Hundreds of Elephants, Thousands of Years

THE NEXT DAY AFTER OUR VISIT TO AJANTA, we went to Ellora, another very famous cave temple site. We rode in the same old Kaiser with the same driver, the same broken springs, and same seating arrangement. We even had the same lunch of canned meat, crackers, and bananas.

We arrived by turning a corner around huge rock outcrops and drove into a dusty area with several ancient trees, many dogs, a few cows, and everything buzzing with flies in the heavy mid-morning heat.

We were at the entrance to a lower plaza, like a canyon, carved out of solid rock at least 50 feet deep. Our driver found a place to park in the shade, and he settled down to watch and wait. Just like the day before, there were just a few other visitors.

In the middle of the carved-out area was an elaborate temple, which had been entirely carved, inside and out, from the native rock, in place. Not just the outside, like a statue, but hollowed out for a huge room inside, too. Hindu pilgrims and tourists like us were slowly filing inside, looking all around, and no one was talking at all.

Buddha mediates at temple entrance

Ellora cave temples with many levels all carved into solid rock

Overhead inside, bats were flying all around, resting on carvings of animals and birds that were the actual ceiling of the temple. The temple was also a cave in its own way because it was cut out from solid rock.

I kept wondering what would have happened if a carver had made a mistake even once among all those thousands of tons of rock and hundreds of years. There would be no repairs made. So, maybe they would somehow have changed the planned carving? But hundreds of nearly identical carved stone elephants were holding up the roof. What a mystery!

Many lifetimes were spent hand-carving all the panels and creatures and building details. How did it get designed, and who kept track of what was to happen? There was nothing here that had happened by chance. For hundreds of years, a master plan was carried out, with careful spacing of all the carved-out monkeys and other animals.

But the workers, the priests, and the designers must have changed from one century to the next. And who were these workers actually, and how was the knowledge of what to do passed down? I began to think back to Chartres, where the two spires did not match. And that was built during just two centuries, not four or five!

As I said, the main center temple's walls and roof were held up by the carved elephants, some of which had been defaced by Moslems after their conquest and had their trunks or a leg missing. I think our guide told us Moslems didn't believe in any representations of living beings, but I was not sure if I had that right.

Many of the statues of Shiva, the main Hindu god, were broken, with heads or arms missing. After the center temple, we next visited the Hindu temples, which was an area of about two acres, with everything cut into the cliff, just as we had seen in Ajanta.

There were also many amazing Buddhist caves like those in Ajanta, which had been carved into the valley wall. Here, these caves were used by monks to live in, and to work and to pray, as well as for temple activities. The walls were carved stone, part of the mountain rock, including intricate screen-like lattice details, also all from the same bedrock. Some carved plaster was added later.

Hundreds of stone elephants hold up temple alter

It was really hard to describe the feeling of entering inside the rock like this. The interior was elaborately carved with gods and ornaments. I felt that, although there was no one living here, and no one had lived here for more than 100 years, the temple spaces were not empty. There was something here besides rock and damp air. Even after years of being abandoned and misused, there were still hints of ochre yellow and cinnabar-like red painting decorating on the temple walls.

It got very hot in the cutaway canyon area as the high noon sun approached, and there was no breeze at all. I had to keep reminding myself that it was winter here and still so hot! The only shade in the temple area was inside the damp cool caves themselves.

Looking up we could see the grassy edge of the cutaway plateau above. If we had gone there, the whole temple and cave area would have been invisible, only marked by the huge cutaway hole.

We had a picnic in the shade of a large tree among more than a dozen dogs. A curious little boy watched us, too. He would not take any food because it was against Hindu religious rules to eat or take any food that Moslems or Christians have touched. And vultures were always watching for scraps, too.

After lunch we went back to the caves and saw another Jain temple. Jains worshipped the end of many reincarnations, when the soul would finally return, instead of worshiping gods. It was the oldest religion practiced at these temples, where their holy men lived long before Buddha's time. Jain, Buddhist, and Hindus all worshipped here side by side for hundreds of years, sharing a holy site until the Moslem conquest. Even then all four religions used the location for a while.

After the long ride back to Aurangabad, still on Chris's lap, with the car swaying on its broken springs, we all had late afternoon naps under the rattan fans in our rooms. When we sat down for dinner, it was roast mutton and crispy roast potatoes this time, with canned peas. And for dessert there were cut up oranges with custard. We cannot drink the water here or anywhere in India. But, as a treat, we had British-style ginger beer, which is like ginger ale but spicier.

As soon as the sun went down, it got dark and cooled off very quickly. Like a light switch, suddenly it was nighttime. Mary said this was because we were closer to the equator and also in an area that was almost a desert.

January 31 - Waiting for Prince Sihanouk

WE GOT UP LATER THAN USUAL, about nine, and after an English breakfast of eggs, toast, marmalade, and stewed fruit, we went to the Aurangabad Fort. There were about 1,000 steps up, around and through the Mogul arches; the walls rose like the cliffs below the Parthenon in Athens. Looking out from the top, I saw barren dusty land with dried grasses and ox carts on lanes between fields that were not planted and some plateau-like land areas rising up like tables.

I kept thinking back to when this place was many days on horse-back from the next fort. There was no sign of water anywhere that I could see. But there must be springs somewhere!

We had a snack of bananas and crackers in the Mogul tomb and then went back to the hotel in Aurangabad but had to stop in the driveway. We had to wait for the Cambodian Prince, Mr. Sihanouk, who was also the Prime Minister, to finish eating his endless long breakfast of pears and kumquats. He had a whole entourage of his staff and family with him and three well-armed bodyguards, too.

They had new-looking black Mercedes cars with tinted windows, air conditioning, and small flags on the front fenders. Prince Sihanouk was here to visit the temples, too, but while he was at the hotel, no one could enter or leave. We just sat in the shade in front of the hotel, watched over by his bodyguards for what seemed like forever.

We had to move away from the buildings when the prince came out. Then we could go to our rooms, to pack, rest, and then have lunch.

Late in the afternoon, the ever-faithful Kaiser with our driver took us to the airport, along with the old Hudson full of our luggage. In the airport shed, one man in a white shirt was taking tickets and tagging the bags with paper tags where he wrote BOM in pencil.

It's the only place they fly to from here. The young boys put the bags on a wagon and waited for the plane, along with the rest of us.

There was a short grass runway that they lit at dusk with kerosene torches which we saw when we came in a few days ago. One DC-3 would come in and out each day. Otherwise, it was an open field of dead grass and sleeping dogs stretched out in the shade here and there at the sides, as well as cows looking around with blank stares.

We got to bed (north of Bombay) at about 12:30 a.m.

February 1 - Sun and Sand

We had a quiet day at the Sun and Sand, a beach resort on the coast north of Bombay after getting in after midnight from Aurangabad. We sat by the pool, ordered sandwiches and drinks. Our parents had said that since we would be traveling for the next three weeks, it would be good to have a quiet day.

Older, overly tanned English or American women lounged about the pool, including one woman whose leg flesh sagged way down from her too-tight bathing suit. Chris rolled his eyes and smiled a little. There were also airline stewardesses on stops between flights, including groups from Pan Am and another group from United Arab Airlines.

It was hot, humid, and still. Flies were buzzing. We ordered cold drinks like fresh orange juice and iced tea with lemon, mint, and lots of sugar. Indians mostly drank hot tea even in hot weather, and usually with milk and lots of sugar in the English style. I liked it that way, too, in the morning.

Indian women and men were not using the pool at all, just foreigners. Maybe they did not like to take their clothes off in public.

We went for a swim in the Indian Ocean. It was calm and murky, and really warm. Not really refreshing. Mary swam a few strokes and then went back to the pool. I saw toilet paper floating by. Just offshore there were many wooden fishing boats drifting, their dark sails completely limp. More fishing boats dotted the whole ocean all the way out to the horizon.

In the late afternoon we went back to the airport and took an Indian Airlines Boeing 707 to New Delhi. It had the red Air India lettering on it because, Arthur told me, that was who actually owned the plane. But the pilots wore Indian Airlines shirts and jackets because Indian Airlines was basically renting the plane until they could get some bigger planes of their own.

February 2 – The Best Part of Our Day

We were going to be in New Delhi for a few days, so Duncan and I unpacked our clothes, and Mary arranged for some laundry to be done. We did arithmetic and spelling lessons in the morning and had a swim after lunch in the hotel pool. It was even hotter here than in Aurangabad, but there was air conditioning and a swimming pool!

Chris was going to test us tomorrow on spelling lists and arithmetic tables as he did almost every week. Then, he would send these to our home teachers at the Calvert School in Baltimore. Chris always discussed all of this with Mary, and I guess everything was okay. Duncan and I hardly ever heard anything at all about the Calvert teachers. I don't think Chris was sending our themes to her because they were not required. But they were the best part of our school day, at least for me.

Actually, we did get one letter that I remember from the teacher when we were still in London, and she said everything was okay. She probably did not have any pictures of us or know anything about the places we were going, but Mary insisted that we do the work and take the tests so we wouldn't have to repeat this year when we got home!

I had seen a lot of temples, palaces, and ruins in the past month, and I was told there were lots more to come. So many different people, languages, designs, and religions!

That first evening, I did not feel well so I stayed in the room at dinner time. Maybe I was having what our parents called Delhi Belly. Chris and Duncan came up to check on me. We had been traveling a lot and sitting in hot cars and bouncy airplanes flying through bad weather, and I got sick from those things.

Food was ordered for me but did not come until almost ten o'clock. The waiter at the door woke me up just as Duncan and our parents came up from their late dinner. Anyway, chicken and rice and cold ginger ale were always a good choice for me.

February 3 –Tuglacabad

AFTER A FEW HOURS OF ARITHMETIC AND SPELLING LESSONS in the morning, and lunch at the hotel, we went by taxi in the afternoon to Tuglacabad, south of New Delhi. The area around the fort was so rocky, barren, sandy, dusty, and dry that my eyes turned the very few scrubby trees into ghosts that seemed to disappear and make the ground look even more parched than before.

Along the way there and back were areas with houses and street-lights right next to whole mazes of shacks and piled crates and corrugated metal, where thousands of people lived.

I think Mary arranged with the driver to come back for us after our visit to the fort. He was a tall man with a turban and nodded quietly. The car was a Mercedes I think but had lots of miles on it. Still, it was much newer than the Kaiser in Aurangabad!

The fort was really huge, and the walls were at least 40 feet high. The many arched openings at the ground level inside reminded me a little of Ajanta but built up, not carved out, and much taller.

The Moguls (same as those in Aurangabad) built their buildings by inlaying rocks of all different sizes which don't fit that well, into the mortar and then putting plaster over it. For a while, masonry walls made this way would not make much of a difference. Later, though, as years went by, and especially with earthquakes, they would start to crumble and fall to pieces. The fort, of course, was not actually that old. Roman walls, though, even the ruins, were still nearly as solid as they were in Caesar's time, after 2,000 years.

All the Moguls, including Tuglaca, built fine palaces and forts with their huge wealth from conquering India and taking the gold and jewels. As most kingdoms seemed to do, like the Ottoman's, they got extravagant as they got richer and inlaid everything with jewels and precious stones. Some areas of the fort had been ornamented in this way with special tiles and stones. I really liked the decorated tiles and colors.

I got very thirsty but we did not have anything to drink. Then we saw a camel being used for drawing water, walking slowly around the well to pull up the bucket from way down in the ground. I do not know how far down they had to go for water, but the camel was walking in circles for a long time, and still, there was no bucket and no water by the time we left.

Mary said we would be seeing more forts like this when we got to Agra and other stops in India. The Moguls built hundreds of forts!

We had dinner at the hotel because we did not go out at night now in the big cities because it was hot and maybe too dangerous. Anyway, our parents did not like spicy food and neither did I. Baked chicken with rice was usually okay. The rice had a slight flowery smell, which was very nice. It made for a softer and slightly sweet taste that fit together with the spices, even though it was just plain rice.

February 4 - Levitation is Real

WE DID OUR WRITING, SPELLING, AND ARITHMETIC LESSONS in the morning, again. I wrote in my red notebook about visiting Elora, with everything carved out of solid rock by four different religions over more than 1,000 years.

After lunch at the hotel, chicken sandwiches again, we went to Humayun's tomb (another Mogul emperor), which has a center octagonal funeral room. Here, copies of the burial tomb inscription plaques were kept in the crypt below, so visitors could visit them without disturbing the dead, I was told.

Farther on we saw the place where Gandhi, known as the "father of modern India," had been cremated. It was a simple place, with a simple marker written in Hindi and in English. People were visiting, praying, and leaving flowers.

We stopped to see the New Delhi Red Fort on the way back. We were told that this was built in the 1600s at the height of the Persian/Mogul empire, by the same emperor and same architect as the Taj Mahal.

Standing on the upper level, looking out over the acres of red dusty ground, I saw something that looked like a hut or sedan chair on a platform. A light breeze lifted and shifted the fine red sand, which rose up in small spirals, making the light almost pink.

It appeared that one adult at each end of the platform was holding it with two hands. There was a white canopy overhead, and a man was playing sad quavering music on a flute. Maybe the adults were chanting and singing but I could not hear everything because it was too far away.

A boy about my age was lying on the platform or litter under the canopy. After a few minutes, the adults let go and the litter with the young boy on it began to lift and shift. The cloth blew under the litter, so I could see that there was nothing at all under there, just the boy, the music, and the wind sweeping the white fabric back and forth. He rose up another two feet, kind of hovered and slowly came down to the ground.

Mary watched very carefully and nodded. "That is levitation," she said. She explained that it was a spiritual practice perfected over thousands of years and was a special holy gift that a few children possessed. She said it was a sacred practice and assured me that it was real. She was a scholar and studied many things, so she always had her facts right.

I had never heard of or seen anything like this, not even in my mythology books. It was amazing. I liked mythology and ancient stories. But this was real and happened in an open dirt plaza in plain view of quite a few people, most of whom paid no attention at all.

February 6 - The Prime Minister Arrives

WE DID OUR LESSONS ALL DAY and took a break for lunch by the pool. Chris had to send another package to the Calvert School the following week, I think, to keep on schedule. In the early evening before dinner time, we watched from an upper inside balcony overlooking the Ashoka Hotel lobby as dignitaries arrived, walking down a long red carpet. The king and queen of Greece were there, with a crown for her, and full naval dress uniform for him.

Prime Minister Jawaharlal Nehru and Indian President Radhakrishnan arrived and walked side by side. United States Ambassador John Kenneth Galbraith (from Harvard we were told) came next in line with his wife. President Kennedy apparently had been appointing many important scholars to be ambassadors, people with knowledge to share with the world and who would be respected.

Then came many other important guys whose names we did not know. Mostly ambassadors, I think.

Mr. Nehru was wearing a long gray tunic buttoned up to his neck, with loose gray trousers and leather dress sandals. Arthur explained that this was traditional attire for men, and paid homage to the country's roots with Mahatma Ghandhi by wearing homespun Indi-an-made cotton clothing, although Mr. Ghandi himself had always worn white. Mr. Nehru was showing an example of living simply and not depending on foreigners. Everyone else wore Western-style suits and clothing. The ladies had white gloves and hats.

But of course, he was meeting with foreign dignitaries who were eager to help India and to make friends with Mr. Nehru. They were having a special formal state dinner at the hotel.

February 8 - Taj Mahal Under a Full Moon

WE PACKED UP FROM OUR NEW DELHI stay at the Ashoka Hotel and took taxis to the airport. We flew to Agra, which was south of New Delhi. The airplane was an Indian Airlines Fokker Friendship, which was made in Holland and which had wings on top of the cabin so I could see everything from my window seat. We flew pretty low so I saw farms and villages, and smoke from fires. The ribbons of roads stretched out in all directions until the smoke and haze made them hard to see.

Taj Mahal in broad daylight

The Taj Mahal under full moon

In Agra, Laurie's Hotel had pretty big rooms with high ceilings and big fans, built all around a courtyard that was planted with trees and flowers. The fans really helped to keep the rooms cool. Except for big city hotels like the Ashoka, there was no air conditioning in India, at least so far.

We were not eating out in India but stayed at our hotels for meals, because we were tired from traveling and the water was not good to drink. Mary said it was safer to be in the hotel after dark. Even so, after dinner we walked just a little way, and saw the Taj Mahal by moonlight. It was a full moon, amazingly, shining down the totally still reflecting pool, making the temple glow.

The temple was made entirely of white marble, including the domes. The main dome was very noticeable to me because it did not come straight down to the roof below but seemed to curl back under a little. That made it feel more than a ball shape, more than just half a ball, and it looked more delicate, too. At the top it was not just rounded but swept back up to a point. Everything here was done by hand by stone carvers, and everything was carried and lifted into place by elephants when it was being built.

It made me think of all the different domes we had seen so far, including St. Paul's in London, the vaults at Chartres, the Pantheon dome, Hagia Sophia, and more. The arch shapes were what made them stand up and also curved over the top of us like the sky does.

We asked Mary if she had planned our trip timing to be here for the full moon, way back home more than a year ago. She smiled but would not say yes or no, so I think that meant yes! She knew things, remembered things, and thought about things that most of us did not. I had seen some pages of her notes from different libraries and documents and it sure was complicated to keep track of all that, especially if the writing was in English, French, and Chinese.

The reflecting pool shone with moonlight, and the pool bottom glittered with coins thrown in for good luck. The image of the temple in the smooth water with the bright moonlight was almost brighter than the temple itself.

The plantings around the Taj Mahal were the best-looking gardens I had seen since visiting Hampton Court back in England. The building really had a lot of inlays. Every surface was inlaid with special stones and patterns. It was almost too much, but still the building's shape was so balanced and peaceful, and also mysterious, in the moonlight.

We had been traveling all day and we were tired, so we went back to the hotel to go to bed. I liked sleeping under the big fans with the sound and feel of a breeze blowing, and the mosquito net was shifting a little, too. Outside, the whir and buzz of night insects rose and fell like a song.

February 9 - Fatehpur Sikri

Jodhabai palace, Fatehpur Sikri

OUR PARENTS HIRED A CAR with a driver so we could visit Fatehpur Sikri, Akbar's capital city, which was lived in for only 14 years after it was finished. Emperor Akbar had many grand plans for this city and others, and he really loved to build things!

It was well preserved because it was used so little, and because it was built by a Moslem ruler after the Moslem conquest, so it was not ransacked. Maybe there had not been any big earthquakes either.

There were stables, a mint for making coins, a treasury to keep the money safe, private apartments for many officials, and a playground for children! This was the first time on this whole trip we had visited an historic building and city site with places made especially for children.

There was inlaid marble and tilework everywhere on the enormous arches of the Mosque entry and dome. The mosque dome had the same more-than-half-a-ball dome as the Taj Mahal. Duncan was especially fascinated with this place, and I liked it, too. I loved the sound of the name, Fatehpur Sikri, maybe because of the three syllables and then two. Or maybe because the last word sounded like "secret."

Another city that Duncan talked about from his reading (and he read a lot) was Mohenjo Daro, which was a 4,500-year-old historic city site in Pakistan. We had been scheduled to stop in Karachi, Pakistan, but the stopover was cancelled. Mohenjo Daro also had the three-plus-two sound in its name, although the cities were built 4,000 years apart.

February 10 - Snake Charmer

ON OUR LAST DAY IN AGRA, we went to the Red Fort in the Old City, which was by far more interesting than the fort in Delhi, except there was no levitation here. The forts were red because of the stone used to make them. The clay for the brick and stucco they used was also red from dust from the same stone and clay for the bricks.

The best and most interesting building in the fort was Jaishankar's palace with balconies and terraces everywhere. The people who lived there could enjoy the outside air from almost any room, but they did not have to go down into the main part of the fort where all the soldiers were. This maintained a space for their family. Only royalty had this, though.

I had been liking the carved columns and covered walkways more and more in these buildings because of the shade they provided while being outside. People could move from building to building without being out in the hot sun, or in the rain if that ever happened! The columns were delicate but also looked strong.

We had lunch back at the hotel, relaxed in the afternoon for a little while, and then walked around Agra late in the afternoon. A gnarled old tree stood in the center of the square, its thick rubbery leaves overhead. Still, the afternoon sun burned down and there was no wind at all. It was this hot even in the middle of winter!

To one side of the tree a man was gesturing to us, and I could see that he had a boa constrictor curled up in a basket at his side. In front was a small straw box to which he pointed eagerly. As Arthur reached into his pockets for coins, the man began to play a haunting, sad tune on his flute using only one hand.

Snake charmer in the square

Slowly, the snake lifted its head up, tongue slipping in and out. It wrapped its body around the man's back and chest, up around his neck, and finally, the snake's head appeared above the man's turban like a live ornament. The whole time he was touching the snake's skin.

These snakes killed their food by squeezing and strangling it, so this looked really scary to me. But the man was very calm, and the snake seemed mostly like a dancer. I guess they both have had a lot of practice at doing this. I wondered how you learn to be a snake charmer, and what happens if you make a mistake?

He reached up and stroked its neck where it was right next to his own. His head, and the snake's head, were perfectly still and right next to each other. As he played another song, still very mournful, the snake slowly wound itself back into its basket, while coins from other bystanders clinked into the straw box.

We were then crowded by holy men that Arthur calls sadhus, and also beggars in rags, their bony arms outstretched for baksheesh. Dark eyes pleading and lips murmuring—it was hard to watch, and I could not look at them. The begging never stopped in towns or crowded places. We wanted to visit the market but decided to go back to the hotel instead and rest before dinner. The hotel garden was very calming for me. We had a lot of traveling coming up.

February 11 – Death and Dawn on the Ganges

W E HAD ARRIVED IN B ENARES in the late afternoon. It was hot and still. We had dinner at Clark's Hotel where we were staying. Chicken stew with rice for me; no surprise there! This version had just a little curry spice, and some sweet chutney on the side. We went to bed early while our parents and Chris had drinks in the hotel courtyard bar, which was right below.

Just before dawn the next morning, there was a soft double knock on the door of our room that woke both of us up. A key turned the latch and a kindly tall man in traditional white cotton dress and sandals walked in, bowed slightly, and said: "Young sahibs, it's the time of your journey."

He left a woven tray with two white cups, a pot of steaming hot tea, sugar cubes, condensed milk, and buttered toast with a jam pot on the small round mahogany side table with a white cloth draped over it.

My brother and I sat up under the white cotton covers, under the mosquito netting which swayed slightly from the slow turning of the rattan-blade fan above us, and we swung our legs out onto the wooden floor. In the Indian interior in the early morning, even before dawn, it could already be hot in late winter and early spring. It was so still that not even a flower petal in the garden moved in the garden outside.

We slipped on our shorts, cotton shirts, and leather walking oxfords, ate the toast that we had smeared with marmalade, and sipped the sweetened tea under the slowly gliding fan before joining our parents on the second-floor balcony hallway. The courtyard gardens spread out below with red-flowered groundcover filling in among the paths, and lush trees with thick leaves stretching up way past the roof edge above us.

Pilgrims and mourners on the ghats, Benares

Leaving the hotel lobby, we rode with a quiet driver in a late 1940s model Hudson. Arthur, the driver, and my brother Duncan were in the front, and I was in the back on the hump, between Mary and Chris. We made our way through the still-dim narrow back streets of Benares, with the car's yellowed headlight beams sweeping slowly across the ancient stucco walls.

We had learned earlier that Benares has been a sacred pilgrimage destination for Hindus for a very long time. Hindus traveled from far and wide to visit, and to cleanse themselves in the holy water of the sacred Ganges River. It was also the place where more fortunate Hindus could come to burn their dead, so the ashes and remains could be spread on the slow, massive Ganges. This tradition had been practiced for more than 1,000 years.

During the day, tourists and visitors could walk along the ghats, the stone tiers and steps down to the Ganges, as we did later in the day, and we saw again, the thick brown water slowly swirling by with its remnants of the morning burials all along the river.

But in the earliest light, no one except the Hindu faithful could be present on the ghats. Our driver headed to a pier a little way upstream of the ghats, for our ride in a small river boat to watch the ghats at sunrise from about 100 yards offshore.

Once he cast off the captain was quiet, guiding his boat and the slow thud of the motor out into the main current. His boatman stayed in the bow to handle the lines. A partial canvas top over the stern section gave us some shade, though the sun was not yet up. The captain sat in the middle of the boat with the motor controls and an up-and-down stick to control the steering. He steered by moving the stick forward and back, turning left by pushing it forward, and right by pulling back.

As we turned downstream, parallel to the ghats, the captain turned to us, looking straight at me, as the only photographer, with the Balda camera around my neck, and waved his long index finger back and forth and said, "Sahib: No pictures!" I nodded and looked down. A little later, when he was talking to the boatman, I did take one or two pictures but felt really bad about doing it. They will probably just be smudges in the middle of the picture anyway.

Drifting slowly downstream with the motor off, the captain was silent as the funeral pyres gradually began to burn and release their dense circling smoke into the murky and moist air. The first orange strip of the rising sun crept up over the buildings in the southern section of the city. I could hear the chanting, singing, and wailing among the families, priests, and holy men along the waterfront, where many pyres of scrap wood sticks and paper were lined up and burning.

Otherwise, the world was silent. Faithful Hindus were wading into the river, bending over, and dousing themselves using pottery jugs of water. All the activities of the living had paused on the ghats, and the dead had called their people here to pray and to say goodbye.

After what seemed like a really long time, the captain cranked and started the motor and swung the boat back upstream toward the dock. Arthur explained that all along the more than 1,500-mile course of the Ganges, from the Himalayas to the Bay of Bengal, the river was a holy part of life for everyone in its path. People bathed in it, did laundry in it, dumped their waste into it, fished from it, watered their crops with it, prayed to it, buried their dead in it, and touched it to their lips while praying.

Leaves and branches floated in the river here and there, but almost everything that came to the river was salvaged and used again. The great carp, catfish, and sturgeon that we were told were living in the river, attended to the other remains. Nothing was wasted.

Dense smoke from the funeral pyres hung over the city waterfront, undisturbed by any wind, as it had almost every morning for centuries, holding back the rising sun and its heat, for just a few hours. The captain brought us back to the dock, the boatman tied the bow and stern lines, and Arthur thanked the boatman and captain with quite a few coins.

By the end of our full English breakfast back at the hotel, complete with eggs and toast, all that would be left on the ghats was the last of the ashes being swept into the river by the mourners.

After breakfast, we walked to a nearby park site where tradition stated that Buddha delivered his first sermon. By mid-morning it was crowded, and we were swept up in the chaos and crowd of beggars and priests, sadhus in rags, postcard sellers, rickshaw drivers, and snake charmers.

The park had everything from deer wandering around looking lost to Buddhist monks to Tibetan refugees with their few belongings strapped to their backs. After lunch at the museum in Sarnath, we saw the carved-stone lion column capital shown on some Indian coins. We saw the monkey temple, which is dominated by real live monkeys climbing all around. We had seen them in the wild also in Aurangabad. Sarnath was located where another river joins the Ganges.

We visited the Golden Temple, which was in the middle of Benares bazaar; it had a roof of gold plate. We bought a piece of sandalwood in a shop in the bazaar and rubbed it to get the special smell, which smelled a lot like the incense that the pilgrims were burning on Elephanta Island and on the ghats at dawn, too.

We went back to Clark's Hotel in the late afternoon after a long day. The sour smoke from wood scrap and coal dust cookfires in the alleys, mixed with the drifting remains of the morning's burial pyres, made my throat sting.

February 12 - Welcomed to Kathmandu

WE WOKE UP EARLY IN BENARES for what we had been told would be a long day of travel. We packed up, which we were pretty good at by that time. Laurie's Hotel in Agra had laundered some of our shirts and shorts, so we had clean things to wear after being so hot and dusty. Mary had "drip-dry" light dresses which she washed herself and hung up in the bathrooms almost every night.

We took another Fokker Friendship with the high wings to Padma on the way to Kathmandu. Everyone in the Padma airport was pushing, shouting, and giving directions, so nothing got done for quite a while. There were not enough seats on the plane headed to Kathmandu for the tickets that had been sold. Finally, the DC-3 was ready, and they had seats for all five of us. We climbed aboard on the small steps that folded down from inside the door and up through the cabin to our seats. People were still shouting and gesturing at the airplane as the engines roared to life, puffing lots of smoke at first.

Downtown Kathmandu with Jonny and Duncan

About two hours later we landed in Kathmandu; the wheels went down with their usual thump and whoosh, and the tail of the plane sank little by little as if land were near. But out my window, I saw fields and trees many hundreds of feet below. I leaned and stretched, and could see up through the cockpit door, and out the pilots' windows to the mountains beyond. Then, suddenly, the hard bump of landing as the plateau of the city came up to meet us.

Arthur had told us that India and Nepal were having a border quarrel dating back to the British years in India, and that it had already led to some fighting. The Nepalese were refusing to fuel or service Indian aircraft. But they still wanted visitors to come, and Arthur mentioned that Indian Airlines was the only airline except for the Nepal airline that served Kathmandu. The Nepal airline had

The young Buddha meditating, Kathmandu Temple

one DC-3, and they used it mostly for flights into the mountains, and to the kingdoms of Sikkim and Bhutan. He said that those flights went to places where some people had never seen a car before!

We climbed down the rear stairs of the aircraft and into the mountain air of the Himalayas. Steep hills, valleys, and rock mountains were around us on three sides.

Kathmandu skyline suddenly appears

Soon after, on the other side of the simple shed that served as the airport, an old Jeep station wagon was loaded up with our luggage and the driver took all of us into town and on to our hotel. It was a tight squeeze.

The Snow View Hotel did not have running hot water, so after we got there and settled into our rooms, we washed in the sink down the hall where the toilet was, with pots of hot water brought up from the kitchen. We could not drink the tap water here or anywhere we had been since we left Greece.

A dinner of bowls of steaming hot vegetables and rice was served to us in the dining room at a table made of planks with plank benches. We could always eat the rice because it was boiled.

The beds were planks on handmade frames with simple mats. No soft pillows here! Night came quickly in the mountains in winter, bringing a sudden and deep cool breeze with it. I could hear a river rushing by below my window, and even though the room was not at all luxurious, it was very comfortable in another way.

I had never been to mountains like these. The air was clear and I could almost imagine the huge mountains just outside of town. I drifted off to sleep right away, "before you could say Jack Robinson," to use one of Mary's phrases.

Also, Mr. Medies, the proprietor, smiled at us kids whenever he saw us and was very nice and welcoming to everyone. That helped a lot, too. He had a small, trim beard, and he was getting bald. He busily moved about making sure everyone had what they needed.

February 13 – Mountain Monastery

OUR BREAKFAST CONSISTED OF TOAST, corn flakes (kind of stale from having been shipped halfway around the world in those little boxes), and tea with canned milk. We sat near the inside wall, I guess because it was warmer. On the outside wall, Arthur had us notice four men at a table under the window. They were North Koreans, he said, and he thought maybe they were there on government business. North Koreans do not travel for fun he told us because it was too expensive.

Our parents hired a Land Rover and driver to take us to a Buddhist monastery named Sruviam Buotnathe. It took about one hour to get there. Once there, we saw that the monks were dressed in simple long yellow robes, and some of them looked younger than me. Arthur had studied and written about Buddhism for many years and so was interested to see the monasteries and temples untouched by outside influences from China or India. The monastery was simple and very quiet. It was easy to breathe and relax, but in another moment it kind of took my breath away.

We then went on to Paten in the same Land Rover. Paten is more like a frontier town even though we were told that 20,000 people lived there. It had a long history of travelers coming through from distant places, crossing the mountains from China, from India, and other countries farther to the west.

On every corner and in all the alleys, there were cows and dogs wandering around, and many craftsmen making things. Cows were milling in the street, men were hammering brass in a shop nearby, young children were making pottery on small pottery wheels, and dogs were barking at us and each other. Later, we bought a small clay pot, usually used for temple offerings, and a bronze flower vase from Tibet. It was very detailed with many traditional designs.

Even so, Paten had a quiet feeling that was relaxing for me. Beyond the noise of all the work going on, and the smells of cooking fires and pottery kilns, the sky opened to the mountains and their huge peaks. We saw a "stupa" left by Ashoka when he visited there. The word meant "heap" in ancient Sanskrit, and this type of building was usually used only for burial. We were told some of the stupas near there were older than Buddhism itself.

Our driver took us back to the hotel and we washed up. At our dinner that night, with more vegetables, rice, and lamb, Arthur told us about a side trip he had taken while we were in New Delhi and busy visiting the Red Fort, seeing the levitation, and doing lessons. He told us he had been carrying some small gifts for the Dalai Lama, the leader of Tibetan Buddhism, and he had gone to visit him and bring the gifts. The temples where he lived are in Dharamashala. Arthur was pretty quiet about the details of his visit, but he did say that the Dalai Lama's brother lived in Indiana, and that he had brought some family gifts also.

During that same trip he had visited Chandigarh, which was a brand-new city being built as the capital of the Punjab state, which is where the Sikhs live. Duncan and I were sad not to have seen the modern city designed by the famous architect Le Corbusier. We sure had seen lots of older cities!

A Buddhist monk watches us silently

February 14 - A Bell in the Silence

OUR PARENTS HIRED A DRIVER with a Jeep station wagon, the same one that brought us from the airport, I was pretty sure. We all piled in and headed up into the mountains and away from Kathmandu. We went up a winding sandy road cut into cliffs, with no guardrails at all, headed for a village more than 6,500 feet above sea level. Our parents said we were going up to see a remote village really close to the Himalayas.

Along the way on the right-hand side against the mountainside, many men and women with no shoes were seated cross-legged in the sand ditch that was the road gutter. Every few hundred feet there was a pile of rocks each the size of a large roll or small loaf of bread. Each worker had a deep basket with these larger stones and a smaller flat basket with smaller rocks. They were crushing the big rocks by banging them together by hand and slowly making gravel. They had no shovels or wheelbarrows. Just the clip-clip of stone against stone, faces under wide-brimmed bamboo hats, down-turned against the hot spring sun.

Our driver explained that they were lining the ditch with stones to prevent the road from washing out in monsoon season rainstorms. He said the rains would return in June, so it required lots of workers before it was too late. He said that the year before more than a mile of this road had washed right down the mountainside.

He drove as far as he could until there was no road anymore. He parked and we walked up another one thousand feet on a two-mile trail to a small hilltop village of mud and stone huts. I saw mountains so close by, most of which were more than 20,000 feet tall. Snow was being blown off the peaks like flags or streamers, and the peaks were sticking straight up out of the clouds like axe heads and needles.

We had a picnic of canned meat and crackers packed for us by the hotel, and we ate it in the open central area of this very old and simple village. The villagers hardly noticed us at all. They were attending to their yaks, sheep, and goats. There was nothing for sale here, no stores, no other visitors, no postcard salesmen. Not even a building with glass in the windows. Hungry but friendly dogs circled around us, waiting for scraps.

Himalayan peaks from remote village

While we were sitting there, I heard wind across the valley to the north whistling softly in the tall pine trees. Cowbells tinkled clearly from many miles away. We were all still and silent, listening. Had we heard a voice calling or singing from a temple that was far away and out of sight?

And then, a deep bell rang a few times, maybe from a monastery or temple somewhere far into the mountains, even closer to Tibet. The sound rang in my head for long afterwards. Who or what was calling to us?

Going back down to the car, we were able to walk at a quicker pace. I don't think a truck had ever even been to this village! Everything had to be carried in by people or on the backs of yaks and donkeys.

As we started down the mountain road in the Jeep for the trip back to Kathmandu, the driver turned off the engine. The brakes squealed from metal on metal. Bare cloth was all that was left of the tires with no rubber at all; they slipped back and forth through the sandy ruts. To the right of the car, the sand just spilled away down a steep mountain side for hundreds of feet. Mary and I never liked heights. Her lips were sealed tight and she stared straight ahead. She clutched my right hand while the brakes screeched.

Arthur explained that the driver was saving gas because it was expensive and hard to get. What they called petrol came in from India in barrels carried on two poles by four sherpas. It cost $5 a gallon, about ten times the cost at home, and they don't have nearly as much money as Americans to begin with.

Mud and thatch buildings high in the foothills

At one point, part way down the mountain side, the driver looked at Arthur in the front seat and said that some years earlier the Jeep itself had been carried in from India by sherpas though the jungle. Four sherpas took the wheels off, threw them inside the car, picked up the car and walked up the mountain. That is what he said, because I asked to be sure. This Jeep station wagon was older than the 1940s Jeepster Arthur had when we lived in California!

Once we were down off that sandy mountain road, we came to a camp of Buddhist refugees from Tibet. The shacks were made of rough wood and sheet metal, with wood smoke circling, and children running everywhere. There were strings of colored flags over the doors like the ones we had seen in the street markets of Kathmandu.

Mary explained that the Tibetan families had fled from the Chinese who had invaded Tibet. The refugees had walked here on foot through ice and snow over the very high and rocky mountains. They spoke their own language and it was hard for them here in Nepal. But at least they could be Buddhists and no one bothered them about it, Mary said.

They had their children and a few animals like goats and chickens. It reminded me of the camps in Beirut on the road to Baalbek. I was not sure if the refugees had water and food, or schools for their children. Living was really different, depending on where a person was born.

February 15 - Batgow Palace

We went to the small city of Batgow for a day trip, in the same Jeep station wagon with the same driver as the day before. What was his name? Maybe he never told us.

We went first to the main square where the King of Batgow's palace (about 1400 AD) was. We were told that this palace dated from a time before Nepal was even a country. It had a gold-lined doorway which was not in good condition but was still very beautiful. It was handmade without any machines or modern tools and had been mentioned in the log of a Chinese traveler in the early 18th century, at least I think that is what Arthur said.

We walked all around the square where there were a few shops and many old wooden buildings. There were craftsmen making pottery, brass, and wood items. There were dogs everywhere, mostly friendly, pretty small, and always hungry.

The temple doors and windows had beautiful solid wood carvings around them with lattice-like designs, as well as animal carvings and other ornaments. The roof edges were overhanging and supported by weathered wood carvings from really huge heavy timbers. The pigeons liked them, too, with lots of little crevices!

The king had commissioned the best craftsmen of the time to work on the palace because he himself was a considerable crafts-man in wood, we were told. There were legends of his carvings and handiwork. Such skills were still treasured here, even centuries later, especially from the hands of a king.

We had the same hotel box lunch picnic of canned deviled ham and crackers in the square and then walked back along some of the alleys where artists and wood carvers were making pots and wooden items. The smells of freshly cut wood, of smelting brass and bronze, along with food cooking over dried yak-dung fires, filled the air.

At least this trip did not have the scary mountain roads! There was more of what is called "traffic" here, which meant trucks piled high with wood and hay and pipes and almost anything, and buses full of people with their heads poked out of the windows. The roofs of the buses were loaded as high as the trucks with the travelers' belongings. Otherwise, there were a few more cars and lots of animals everywhere. In an hour or so, we were back in Kathmandu for another quiet dinner at the Snow View Hotel. Mr. Medies was still his smiling self. He wanted to know if we had enjoyed our day. The North Koreans had left by this time.

February 16 – 'John Kennedy!'

AFTER TALKING WITH MARY, Arthur had decided that the planned trip by small plane to the mountain kingdoms of Sikkim and Bhutan was too dangerous. I think it was the weather, and maybe the aircraft maintenance, if there was any. Could we go in the Jeep, I had asked? It would be many days and there might not be any open roads, gasoline, or hotels, he advised. I think he was sad, too. What I knew about Nepal made me want to go farther into the mountains and see places unknown to most visitors. But it was not safe or possible.

Artisans at work in the streets of Kathmandu

We had decided to stay in Kathmandu and to have extra time without any big plans. We explored the city by walking around. We walked a lot. We always walked. I liked not having a plan for everything on a surprise day like this, and to just wait and see what was around the next corner. But I needed grown-ups to be with me most of the time because I was only eleven years old. I was okay by myself in Athens and Beirut for a little while, but this place was not familiar at all.

Kathmandu was a busy, thriving place, being the capital and largest city, with mountaineers and travelers from all over the world. They were speaking German, French, Japanese, and many other languages. We were told that the season for climbing the tallest mountains, like Everest and Annapurna, would be coming soon after the rains, and already, there were climbers putting together their supplies and equipment.

Carpenters sawing planks, Kathmandu

The mountaineers always had local sherpa guides and porters from Nepal, as these men were from here and knew everything about the mountains. And they were so strong and also very careful, I was told. There was so much to know and to admire! Some of the sherpa guides had already climbed Everest more than once.

The streets were full of people and bicycles, cars, trucks, and yaks. There were many buses like we had seen before, topped with boxes, luggage, and supplies, and filled with passengers holding bags and boxes of vegetables, bags of potatoes, and even live chickens in their laps.

We visited several temples, which offered some quiet and where people were praying. We peeked into many shops on the narrow side streets, always greeted with big smiles. The temples were not the special larger ones with guides and people selling postcards. These were mixed in on the small streets where people went alone or with their families or friends to have a quiet time and to pray. No priests or ceremony, just people making their way through the city and stopping in at a temple for a moment of peace.

Our parents bought some small pottery and Tibetan prayer flags like those we had seen at the camps. Earlier, we had a longer breakfast than usual, and then we had lunch back at the hotel rather than a picnic. There was even time for a nap!

In the afternoon Duncan and I went exploring by ourselves along a side street next to the hotel and found several boys our age playing there on the roadside while their mothers were doing laundry in the river just below. The women used the boulders to scrub the clothes clean. It was the same river that we could see from the dining room at the Snow View Hotel. I think Arthur was up above in the dining room keeping an eye on us.

One of the boys ran up shouting "Inglese, Inglese," thinking we were English, and I had been told most white people here were English. Duncan said, "No, we are Americans," and the boy then said "John Kennedy!" They were excited that they knew our president by name and so were we. We talked and played with them at the roadside. Using stones and sticks, we made some small stone structures and had a good time.

Wow, we had other kids to play with for the first time in months! We wrote down each other's addresses on a small slip of paper, and I told them I would write to them when we got home. Mary put the paper into her reticule, in a special pocket that she had where small papers cannot get lost.

February 18 – **Window on the Himalayas**

AFTER AN EARLY LUNCH OF DEVILED HAM SANDWICHES and friendly goodbyes at the Snow View Hotel, taxis took us to the small airport that had seemed to me to be perched at the edge of a cliff. Soon, as we roared down the runway in an Indian Airlines DC-3, the rotary engines were wheezing for air because of the altitude. Slowly the rear tail wheel lifted off the ground and, for a moment, the cockpit aisle rose to level. Then, slowly, the nose went up, the rumble of the tires faded, and the landing gear came up into the wing pockets with a thud.

Even though these were older planes, they were my favorites. We had been flying on them a lot. I had a book about the history of the DC-3, which told the story of how these planes had flown everywhere in all conditions for so many years, and they always came back safely! When I had read the one about using Mazola for the engine oil in the Pacific Islands during World War II, Arthur had just smiled and shook his head. He was a fan, too.

A steep right turn out from the airfield left the hills north of the city just off the front of the plane. Then I could see them briefly from my seat as the airplane continued turning right. After that they disappeared behind us as the pilot set our course for Calcutta more than three hours away. We gained altitude and the ground slipped away below while we slowly climbed, and the sky and clouds seemed to come even closer.

I was seated in a left-side window seat. I always asked for a seat just behind the wing so I could see everything both above and below the plane. I liked to watch the flaps going up and down during landing, and to see how the pilot was steering the airplane, too.

The plane had square glass windows, one per row of seats, and the glass was held in by shrunken, cracked black rubber edges that had pulled back from the joints so the corners were wide open. I could have poked my baby finger through to the outside of the plane. As the cold air roared by, I felt I could touch the mountains.

There was a bank of clouds in the distance off to the left under the Himalayan peaks like a line of pillows. The mountains were saw-toothed into the brilliant blue sky. They were perhaps 150 miles away, but even so they were raw and breathtaking to me and felt so close! Annapurna was a name I had seen on a map and heard spoken, and I could not get it out of my head, as if it were the name of a person I had just met, or maybe a friend from before we moved away.

I began to hum quietly to myself, not overheard because of the roar of the engines and the wind rushing through door and window frames.

It was cold, and the plane was not pressurized, so I wrapped myself up in the worn dark blue blanket provided by the cabin steward. My face stayed glued to the view, each breath making a circle on the window, then that mist faded.

Annapurna was my favorite mountain peak even though I was not sure which peak it was in the massive range. I picked out one just for the moment that matched the particular jutting peak from the postcard I had. I hummed quietly. What was that tune? Was it the chant of a holy man in a Kathmandu temple, or the haunting bamboo flute melody that charmed the boa constrictor in Agra, near the Taj Mahal?

I felt something old and also familiar, something from far away and close by at the same time. What was it exactly, I wondered? Peak by peak, the mountains seemed to carry my voice up and down for more than an hour while we cruised at 9,000 feet.

Gradually the mountains faded behind us, and the air below became murkier, as dusty fields and the smoke of the towns and factories of India came closer. I went to the rear of the plane to use the toilet, after which I pulled the lever, and emptied the bowl out under the tail of the plane, watching the lines of fields and roads passing under the open hole. This reminded me of the train we took to New York last summer!

I stayed for a while, holding the lever and watching through the small hole like it was a movie, listening to the roar. I wondered who lived down there, did they have boys like me in their families, and how hot was it anyway? I began to remember the boys we met on the street in Kathmandu and had played with in the rocks and rubble by the roadside, while their mothers, washing clothes in the nearby river, kept an eye on them.

Then there was a tap on the door, and I realized I had used the only toilet on the airplane for quite a while. I opened the door and kept my eyes down and took my seat again. I think I dozed off a little. Arrival at Dumdum Airport in Calcutta was still miles away.

February 19 - Smoke-filled Streets

AFTER ARRIVING AT CALCUTTA'S DUMDUM AIRPORT, close to the Bay of Bengal, from the mountains of Nepal, we walked into a cinderblock building with rusted steel windows. A wide porch roof overhang provided shade, and this was where the luggage was unloaded from hand carts pulled in from the plane. Soon, we went by our usual two taxis toward the city. There were no buses for tourists because there were no tourists and no families. Just Indian men on business.

It was about five o'clock in the evening and, as we got closer to the city, the air became thick, and the sunlight was darkened to a brownish sour-yellow color.

Our drivers picked their way through the crowded streets with throngs of people slowly surging back and forth. Sacred cows were everywhere and the moment the cows dropped their dung, I saw young children scrambling to collect it. I was told they would dry it and use it for cooking fuel.

Smoldering dried dung and burning waste-coal-dust from the mines made the air thick and bitter tasting. I could feel the fine grit on my tongue and lips. Food was being cooked over these open fires on sidewalks, in the street, and in the dusty parks. Everywhere.

Mary told us that half the city's people had no home except the streets. Three million people were living outside in the city streets in the baking heat, and also in the monsoon rains, which were coming again soon. Packed bodies stretched out into the brown fog ahead of us and behind us, and down every alley. People were shuffling and standing, and darting in and around animals, cars, and trucks. There were thousands of people on bicycles, and everywhere was the loud sputtering of motorbikes and their trail of blue smoke.

Our taxis pulled in under a dark maroon canopy. The hotel doormen had turbans and brilliant dark blue dress uniforms with gold details, and white gloves, as they unloaded the cars. The lobby had mahogany walls just like in Bombay, with heavy deep green curtains and patterned tiled floors. A man with a silver cigarette holder lounged in a velvet chair, chatting idly with an English woman in a long cotton dress, while a servant nearby adjusted the electric fan. I had just walked ten steps into a totally different world.

After we got settled in, drank some bottled water and had showers, we went back to the lobby. Except for the dark-skinned business guests, we could have been in London. For dinner we went to a restaurant called Spence's, which was just around the corner. We picked our way carefully among the smoldering fires, nursing mothers, crying babies, beggars, and bewildered cows. The restaurant, just one heavy-paneled door away from the street, was a very British colonial haunt, with crimson carpets, big ceiling fans, and dark blue velvet drapes. Going out from the hotel and back into the smoke and hunger of Calcutta at dusk made my eyes sting and my heart sink. So much suffering everywhere.

Inside Spence's, well-dressed white people and Indian officials sat quietly at the tables. The five of us sat at a round table covered in linen, with linen napkins and silver knives and forks. I ate chicken with rice and our parents shared a bottle of French wine after the customary martinis. That wine had traveled a long way through the tropics on a ship to get here!

When it came time to leave India, after one night in Calcutta and a few days of play and rest to the south of the city in Orissa state, in the town of Puri on the coast, we found ourselves being held back at the airport. Apparently, our typhus shots had expired in the many months since we had left home. In a back room, a kindly gentleman offered to take payment from Arthur to change the vaccination cards, or to administer additional doses to us. Arthur took the medicine choice.

I dreaded the typhus shot because it had been the worst of all the pre-trip shots. But none of them, and there had been more than 20, were easy.

The man took out a needle from his desk drawer, wiped it with a cloth and some alcohol, and we each had our turn. It was dull and it hurt. But there was no reaction other than a red swollen spot. Maybe there was no medicine in the needle after all.

Southeast Asia

February 22 - Sailing in Rangoon

WE FLEW IN FROM CALCUTTA on a Vickers Viscount four-engine propeller plane owned by Union of Burma Airways. Vickers was a British company that made almost all the British airplanes.

Driving into the capital, Rangoon, from the airport, the center of the city that we saw was very cold and hard with modern and grand government buildings with lots of glass. There were wide tree-lined streets but not much going on. The hotel was also modern. There were policemen on almost every corner. Mary said the army was running the country.

The next day, the American Embassy had arranged for my brother and me to go sailing on a lake near Rangoon. It must have been a British officers club or something like that at one time. The small sailing dinghy they gave us drifted across the lake without much wind, toward an island with a beautifully landscaped house. As we drifted closer, soldiers suddenly appeared along the shore with their rifles; two of them came down to the dock and started yelling, their guns pointed at the sky over our heads. We managed to paddle farther out into the lake and caught a light breeze back to the sailing club dock.

We learned later that this was the private house of the dictator of the country, and we had drifted much too close inside the secured zone! Even though we were pretty good sailors, without any wind no one could control the drifting. The people at the club did not say anything and hardly seemed to notice. Maybe it happened all the time. Our parents did not seem to be worried. Anyway, we were hardly ever scolded, and we had done our best.

I loved hearing the water gurgle under the bow of the boat even for a few minutes at the end of our sail, but it also made me a little homesick for our sailing at home. We would be back home in June, so it was still a long time. The harbor at home right now was probably full of chunks of ice.

Our next full day was our last in Rangoon and we spent it touring older parts of the city with a car and driver. We visited an interesting open-air food market with lots of beautiful vegetables and flowers everywhere, along with policemen.

Soldiers with guns and helmets were evenly spaced all through the city.

February 23 - Everything by Boat

Busy canal street market, Bangkok

IN THE MORNING, we left Rangoon for Bangkok on a Royal Thai Airlines DC-6-B, which felt like complete luxury after the DC-3s of India. It had four seats across, four engines, and light-tan vinyl seats with dark-blue cloth upholstery. It had fold-down trays and two toilets at the back, not just one. It flew fast and high, and the stewardesses were dressed in wraparound blue silk, with their hair pulled back in a fancy way. They served us juice and cookies and were very polite.

The seat-pocket information was in English, Thai script, and also in Thai but using the letters that we use. The Thai writing was different from any writing I had ever seen, even in India. Mary was very good with languages, and she said it was close to the ancient Sanskrit language but spoken with very different sounds. Many people, including Mary and Arthur, were smoking.

We only stayed two nights in Bangkok. Everywhere there were canals with boats of all kinds. Sampans, house boats, delivery boats, dugout canoes, motorboats, police boats, small fishing boats; everything seemed to move by boat. It was much, much busier than Venice!

Shops lined the edges of the canals, and on the left side during our boat ride was a boys' school, which could be entered either from the canal dock or from the street behind the buildings. We could see inside the rooms where the boys were in school, all dressed in their dark-blue uniforms with white shirts.

The water was thick and brown and swirled slowly. Our tour boat had about eight people on board including us, and a straw-mat-top to keep the sun off. The captain sat in the stern to operate the outboard motor. Since we were a group of five, we often almost filled a car or table or boat wherever we went.

Men and women in small flat-bottomed sampans paddled alongside to sell us everything from hot peppers to watermelon to postcards to dried fish.

Later in the afternoon our parents went shopping for some raw silk to have a dress and jacket made for Mary once we got to Hong Kong. They brought home samples, and the raw silk looked a little like grass cloth but was softer and denser. It was not at all scratchy but actually really smooth even though it was bumpy. I could happily have looked at it up close for a long time because it was not patterned but evenly irregular. The texture was very intricate.

February 25 - Arriving in Phnom Penh

ARRIVING FROM THE AIRPORT to reach our hotel in Phnom Penh's center reminded me of Beirut, which also had a mix of modern and some French feeling, even a bit of a big city like Paris. There were also side streets with older colonial buildings. The French occupation had lasted for more than 100 years and had just ended a few years earlier.

In India and Burma, there were British and American cars, but not here! Citroën ID sedans, a basic model of the car we had rented for our weekend in Beaune, made up most of the taxis. Citroën Deux Chevaux, like the one we rode in for our outing to Fontainebleau, were everywhere, along with thousands of motorbikes and bicycles.

Dignitaries and rich people rode in the back seats of their black Citroën DS sedans, the luxury version, with glass tinted dark, driven by uniformed drivers looking straight ahead without smiling.

We crossed over the Mekong River, which connected most of southern Asia and carried lots of ships, boats, and trade. Our parents said the river provided water for most of the rice fields in several different countries. The waterfront was lined with warehouses and factories, along with houseboats, sampans, and small sailing and fishing boats. Farther on, there were ocean-going freighters, some with logs piled on deck.

The street signs were in French and also in Khmer script, which was the language they spoke here. It was different from Thai and Hindi. Police at intersections wore dark-blue uniforms, lighter blue berets, polished shoes, gold buttons, and gold epaulets, even in the stifling heat. The army was also very visible on almost every city block, mostly as pairs of men in khaki uniforms with dark forest-green berets, and lots and lots of guns.

These looked like the same guards we had seen with Prince Sihanouk when he was enjoying his fruit at our hotel in Aurangabad during his visit to the famous cave temples.

There were wide boulevards with grassy islands in the middle, planted with tall trees and flowers. Everything was perfectly straight, formal and clean. Everything was very calm, although Arthur had told us that ten years of independence had been full of fighting and chang-es of government. He told us we would just be staying for one night.

February 26 - The Ancient World of Ankor Wat

WE LEFT PHNOM PENH EARLY IN THE MORNING after a continental breakfast, which included croissants and jam! We took our flight to Siem Reap aboard a Royal Air Vietnam DC-3. The pilot spoke to us in Khmer and also in French, and Mary roughly translated because I always wanted to know exactly what was going on, how long it would take, and how high we were going to fly.

Our parents had said that when we go to our new school back home next year, we will be learning French, because it is the interna-tional language, even more than English, and it is also the language of diplomats.

The plane climbed to a low altitude and leveled out over the endless green jungle below, with spaces between the trees for rivers and lakes, and here and there, a road. The villages were just folds in the blanket of trees.

After landing at Siem Reap airport, we were taken by two cars to the town of Siem Reap near the temples that we had come to see. We collapsed into the worn cloth upholstery of the Citroën ID sedan.

These were older versions of the DS sedans we rode in back in France and Lebanon, and also in Phnom Pehn just in the last few days. They had the same unusual steering wheel where the column came up and turned out and became the only spoke, for a continu-ous steering wheel.

The back of the car could go up and down with air for more space underneath on a rough road or for ease of getting in and out. They were a far cry from the Jeeps of Kathmandu or the Hudsons of India, and even the brakes seemed to work pretty well!

Mary described Siem Reap as a centuries-old market town for the surrounding villages and jungle area and said that it was becoming a tourist town because of the temples and ruins. For hundreds of years the temples were nearly forgotten, hidden, and wrapped in jungle until they were rediscovered not that long ago.

Arthur and his lion, Ankor Wat

Arthur said that the temple complex at Ankor Wat was the largest religious structure anywhere, in the whole history of the world. That was a big statement, but he usually had his facts right. The temples were built by a powerful Khmer emperor and honored many Hindu gods and goddesses.

Mary and Arthur at a Khmer temple
preserved as it was at re-discovery 50 years earlier

The road into town was completely straight and went on for what seemed like miles and miles. It was lined with tall trees something like what we saw in Italy. Arthur said that this was how the French built roads in their colonies.

We passed only two or three cars and only one truck coming the other way.

February 27 - Temples in the Jungle

Our hotel, the Auberge des Temples, was several low buildings with wide overhangs for shade nestled down into the jungle. There were lots of lush plants with red and yellow flowers all around the courtyard in front of the rooms. Maybe just because of its name, the hotel seemed a little more French than Cambodian, with French and Khmer writing on the signs, the day's menus written in French on the chalkboard, and French being spoken at the front desk.

On our first day, after a breakfast of good French bread and cassis jam, we went to Ankor Wat. Ankor Wat had been covered in jungle for 400 years and had been losing its battle against the trees and vines. It kept crumbling until about 1900, when some Frenchmen rediscovered it. That was only 60 years ago! I wondered if they knew it had been there all along? The people here must have known about the huge shapes in the jungle, and maybe remembered stories?

Once inside the first wall with gates and sculptures guarding it, we crossed a wide, shallow moat used for water storage to flood the rice paddies, but not for protection. Beyond, there was another wall and some lakes, and then another wall and grass areas and steps up to the central temples.

It sounds confusing, but it was a peaceful and beautiful place, with no sounds of trucks or machinery at all. Puffy clouds slowly went by overhead, and there was a light wind. No rice was growing, but big long-legged birds were walking around in the shallow water, bending over to eat. When we finally got to the entry of one of the main shrines, it was interesting because many religious figures carved around it were watching the doorway. They were beautiful figures, especially from the Rama Yana (Hindu Book), is what Arthur explained. The carvings included monkeys, elephants, fantastic animals, and people and gods all in the most exotic and twisted positions.

Even though the jungle had torn at the stone buildings and decorations, some of it had been put back together very carefully with the original pieces. That must have been very hard work, because the jungle vines and roots were really strong, and they grew fast because it was so warm and wet in this part of the country.

We had lunch back at the hotel, a very French meal even though we were really far from France. It included Potage a la Maison (soup), entrecote (beef steak) grille, pommes frites, haricots verts (green beans), and glace vanille. There were pictures on the walls, mostly photographs from early explorations of Ankor, showing the huge trees climbing out of the temples.

Later in the afternoon, we went on the so-called "short circuit" of temples close by. Our transportation was by motorbikes with trailer carriages fastened behind, called motorized rickshaws. Traditional rickshaws have a man running between poles to pull the light wooden two-wheeled carriage. But that would never have worked in the soft sands here in the jungle.

Duncan and I shared one, and the grown-ups each had one. We saw some unfinished temples that had been left half built. No one seemed to know why the builders left them unfinished, but I was going to keep asking. The Khmers did not leave any books, or at least not that I had heard about.

Mostly, these temples were smaller but of similar construction to Ankor Wat. We also saw a temple that was left as it had been found, with trees growing up the spires and trees lifting the huge wall stones like they were light as feathers. This will help visitors like us in the future to understand how the jungle tried to tear down these buildings. It was amazing to see huge stones lifted by roots like that, as if they were just small rocks on the beach.

We were brought back to the Auberge in time for a rest before dinner and the fast-falling darkness.

February 28 - Riding on Elephants

BY THE MIDDLE OF THE MORNING, a while after breakfast and a little rest time on the hotel veranda while our parents had more coffee and we were watching for monkeys, our parents had arranged again for motorized rickshaws to take us into the jungle, this time on what was called the "big circuit."

There were so many temples and structures buried in the jungle! I cannot remember all the places we went to. These temples were older, deeper in the jungle, and more massive than any of the others except Ankor Wat. I tried to imagine this area of hundreds of square miles in its heyday, with roads, temples, markets, and people growing rice and vegetables.

The trails through the jungle were sandy and soft as we were in the dry season, and the motorbikes skidded along in the soft surface, kicking up sand and blue smoke into the rickshaw carrier with its extra fat bicycle tires. The flying sand stung my legs because I was wearing my blue shorts and sandals.

The rickshaw had a hard varnished wooden seat, which Duncan and I also shared for this trip. Trees towered overhead and we kept looking for more monkeys. We saw them in the temples, but not in the trees here. Arriving at the remote temples with their great walls fallen and overgrown, moss everywhere, and strips of tree roots twisting high up on the stone stairs, was like falling back into a dream after waking in a sweat.

Then, in an open sandy clearing just beyond, there were several elephants with benches high up on their backs. We were told we would ride on them from here on because the roads were too soft for rickshaws. I climbed a ladder up and up, to be close to the top and the driver. As I climbed, the elephant turned his head to look at me with his brown silky eyes, snorted with his trunk and lightly tapped one foot. His big ears slowly waved away the flies.

I continued up the last steps of the ladder onto the passenger bench, which had a colorful red and yellow cloth on it and a delicate wooden rail just a few inches high on three sides. The seat was flat, but underneath it, the wood was shaped to form over the elephant's body like a saddle and strapped beneath its belly.

Jonny with grim smile while hanging on for dear life

Suddenly, after quiet clicking and spitting sounds from the driver, the elephant began to walk. The driver was up front, riding on the elephant's neck, with his legs behind the big, battered, fly-covered ears. We were up on the shoulders, and what shoulders a 2,000-pound elephant had! With each step the chair platform rocked heavily from side to side like a rowing dinghy in a big swell.

Slowly, slowly we walked and rolled into the jungle as motion sickness crept up on me. The heat, the smell of the animal, the smell of the driver, and the sun breaking through the towering treetops above all combined to make me feel sick. Of course, Mary pointed things out constantly, which made it all worse. When we finally reached the next temple after about 15 minutes, I sat in the shade and drank a bottle of French Evian water. We could not drink any water except the bottled kind. French products, customs, and practices were still everywhere. Anway, being still and having water did help.

This temple, called Phnom Bakheng, had amazing carvings of animals and also roof-top areas like drip castles at the beach. When it was time for the trip back, I think we went along a different path, past some other temples and through an even denser jungle area. The tall trees hung their branches and vines down so far that I could almost reach them with my hands! This part took a lot longer. I think I was getting used to the motion, because it made me sleepy during the trip back.

Eventually the first big clearing came into view, with our rickshaws and their drivers standing around smoking those French cigarettes with the blue wrapper. It was good to get back on the ground, with only flying sand and pebbles, and gasoline smoke to worry about.

March 1 – 'We Don't Pay for Water in Wichita!'

AFTER OUR USUAL AND DELICIOUS FRENCH BREAKFAST, we all went to Ankor Thom, a whole ancient city dating from about 850 AD, which was about two miles away from the Auberge. It was built as the capital city of the Khmer empire by Jayavarman VII and then expanded by later descendants in his family dynasty. Even though Arthur studied the history of cities, Mary seemed especially excited to go on this visit. Maybe she had had enough of temples and jungles?

The old city was built along the Siem Reap River, which was connected with moats that surrounded the city. I don't know if they used boats because I didn't see any in the carvings, but they must have. There was a bridge made of carved lions, and many temples and palaces, as well as ruins of areas where there had been offices and houses for the emperor's staff and family.

Unlike Ankor Wat, which was not fortified against attack because it was really one huge temple with water reservoirs for growing food, Ankor Thom was planned and located for protection and for easy access by travelers. Its gates were facing basically north, east, south, and west, and from these gates, roads were built that led throughout Jayaraman's kingdom.

It was not hard at all to imagine oxcarts creaking along, filled with big sacks of rice, holy men traveling barefoot dressed in rags, and children running all around, all mingled together in this city for many centuries, more than 1,000 years ago.

When we got back to the Auberge, we had a nap and had to wait for dinner because the French ate dinner late. Our parents had some wine while we waited. Just as we sat down for our dinner of rice with vegetables and pork, which was both a little sweet and a little salty, a familiar voice rang out in the hotel dining room. "What do you mean we have to pay for water. We don't pay for water in Wichita!" An American tourist lady was waving an Evian bottle at the dining room manager who was smiling politely. Her companions were trying to calm her down, but she kept going on and on with her complaint.

The thing was, we recognized this voice instantly, because we had crossed paths with this woman and her tour group in Istanbul, where she had made a scene about the food at our hotel dining room. She had surely been home to Kansas since then, and was now on some tour probably called "Jewels of the Orient" or something catchy and stupid like that. Arthur, after raising his left eyebrow the way he does when something is not quite right, had named her "Bessy Jerk." Here she was again.

Were they following us? Boy, I hoped not! I wanted to hide under the table. At least we did not have to put up with her in Nepal and all over India. Arthur gave the manager a kind smile. After all, that Evian water had spent two months on a ship to get here from France. She could have had water from the sink, but it would probably have made her sick. Then she would have had to stay in her room. Gee, that would really have been too bad.

March 2 - Lost and Found

AFTER GETTING A FULL VISIT TO ANCHOR THOM, I thought we had seen everything and soon we'd be getting back on our travel plan. But Duncan kept talking about Banteay Srei and I kept asking him what it was. Mary filled in the gaps at dinner at the Auberge, which included a French-style carrot soup with potatoes that reminded me of being at the Hotel St. Simon in Paris. I could not figure out how they could make that crusty French bread here in the jungle, but it sure was good. The next day's trip was planned over dinner but I did not listen too much because I was busy eating.

The next morning, when we got to Banteay Srei, it seemed so different from all the temples we had visited around Ankor. First of all, the temples were smaller. There were a lot of temples restored and also many still buried in the jungle just visible as huge garden lumps. The buildings we could see were what was left over after the regular houses and buildings were long gone. Many of those had probably been made of wood. We had seen termite nests here that were the size of refrigerators. The termites cleaned up everything, including whole buildings.

Banteay Srei had been restored, and the buildings here had been used by families who were not kings and royalty even though they were very rich. Mary wanted to see the Temple of the Women (I guess it could be translated as Goddesses, too), and it still had its stone roof and beautiful carved stone overhang guarding and protecting the entrance. Inside there was a small chamber, and it seemed like it was still being used. Pilgrims had been coming and going, which was true of many of the historic places. There were people in ragged shirts and some in dark suits, children in fancy dress and some dressed in barely more than rags.

Ruined and restored temples and grounds, Banteay Srei

There were dozens of brass and pottery plates of food offerings along the wall, a bit like our visit to Elephanta, and outside, there were flowers on the steps, left as thank- you gifts.

For centuries these buildings were buried in jungle, but now they were restored enough so they felt like buildings more than ruins, and pilgrims were using them as if they had never stopped using them from more than 800 years ago. Even though the buildings were buried and forgotten for over 400 years, it seemed like they never stopped being real and alive. It was now all the same again, as it had been long before. Pilgrims were bringing offerings, giving thanks, and praying, as they had for so many centuries.

The buildings had been lost and then found again, and since people like us also knew this, it was as if they had been there full of life all along. That is something about history, that it does not stop and start. It continues no matter what.

March 3 - Canceling Vietnam

AFTER WE HAD GOTTEN UP AND HAD BREAKFAST, our parents told us about another change of plans. We got packed to return to Phnom Penh, where we would spend the night and then go on to Hong Kong. Our stop in Saigon, Vietnam, had been cancelled because it was not safe. Mary was pretty sure that there would be a war there very soon, so they changed our plans.

On our flight aboard a Royal Air Cambodia DC-4, which had four engines, we retraced our course not quite as slowly over the miles and miles of jungle. The crew served us canned but fresh-tasting orange juice.

Traveling was tiring with all the packing and unpacking, getting used to different places, different beds and pillows, and different bathrooms. It was interesting but a lot of work. Duncan and I have been getting good at it, and we have not left behind anything important.

We had not been doing much for lessons, but Chris said we would be "back at it" when we got to Hong Kong. Still, we had been studying ancient ruins and culture, not just sitting around playing checkers, eating candy bars, or reading comics.

Going to Hong Kong was exciting because it was mostly an English-speaking city, and it was still really just another part of China. It would be as close to China as we could get. I did not know much about bigger cities before this trip, but by now I really liked visiting cities of all kinds.

Hong Kong

March 7 – Buses, Bicycles, Boats

Busy Kowloon street

THE TRIP FROM PHNOM PENH to Hong Kong was my favorite flight so far. Cathay Pacific was the Hong Kong airline, and they really made us feel welcome on board the Lockheed Electra II. This was the same airplane we flew on from Amsterdam to Paris. These were turbo-prop airplanes, and I asked Arthur if that meant a jet-propelled propeller engine. He said "Well, not exactly." So, maybe. But they whine when they start up, not putting and smoking like the DC-3s! I was still unclear about what a turbo-prop was, but I planned to keep asking.

The Chinese in Hong Kong were famous for their food and hospitality, apparently. We had tender chicken, potatoes, fresh green beans, and ice cream for our lunch on the plane. The grown-ups had Manhattans "on the house." I did not know they even liked that drink! Maybe it tasted better when it was free?

We arrived in Hong Kong in mid-afternoon and took taxis from the airport in Kowloon toward our hotel, which was also in Kowloon. Kowloon is the mainland part of the Hong Kong colony. The trip was slow through the frantic city pace, down streets jammed with carts, buses, bicycles, motor bikes, construction trucks, police cars, and people walking everywhere. Street vendors were calling out and offering dumplings, roasted meat on sticks, and sweet buns. The sweet and spicy food smells coming from the carts mixed with harbor air and also fried fish.

Life on the Kowloon waterfront

I looked up, and right out the right-side window of the taxi, as we inched along the harbor-front road, was a new building under construction. It was about 15 stories tall. The entire outside was wrapped in bamboo scaffolding, ladders, and rails. All the way up. Men were mixing mortar on the ground, using a rope and pulleys to lift the mixture in baskets way up to where teams of men were laying bricks and mortar.

The scaffolding looked like a forest of wood with the vertical and horizontal bamboo woven together almost like a coarse cloth. All the joints were tied with woven bamboo strapping, strong enough to hold men, mortar baskets, and stacks of brick!

Soon it would be a modern brick-and-glass tower, and it was being made quickly and efficiently using the old-fashioned methods and tools.

The harbor had many ships at anchor, some badly rusted, listing, and seemingly abandoned, and also small freighters. Smaller ships were preparing for trips to places like the Portuguese colony of Macao nearby, I was told, as well as motorized junks, sampans, and almost anything that would float. Mary told us Macao had many casinos for gambling. Chinese and English people, and visitors from all over Asia liked to go there.

Along one older pier I saw houseboats tied up three or four wide, laundry hanging out, and smoke from cooking fires curling up from metal chimneys.

A beautiful, varnished wood motor launch swept by while we were stopped in traffic, with several men in dark suits sitting elegantly in the finely fitted cockpit of the yacht. The captain guided the boat among the small craft going pretty fast, with exhaust curling up from the stern, and the harbor water rolling smartly off the chrome trim on the bow.

As the traffic thinned a little, we worked our way up a steep road toward our hotel. The Hong Kong Carleton Hotel was a modern building, almost on a cliff, facing out toward the harbor and Hong Kong Island beyond, with balconies and beautiful views.

The road continued on up past the hotel, leading to the New Territories. This was an addition of land rented to the British Hong Kong government by China, enlarging the original trading colony set up by the British. Mary had more details, but that was most of it.

Our bedrooms all had beautiful views. Soon, our parents and Chris were enjoying their cocktails overlooking the harbor and

Hong Kong Island, so busy, although right here it was quiet except for the road noise. Duncan and I had ginger ale, but sometimes we had orange juice with soda water. Out over the water, but at our balcony level, I saw planes coming down to land at the airport on the other side of Kowloon.

Mostly, I liked to watch boats and ships moving around down below. I liked thinking about the sailors, the cargo, and what their time at sea was like. I was only one-and-a-half years old the last time we traveled on a ship, from Yokohama to San Francisco, and most of what I could remember was about where we slept, which was on metal beds separated by curtains.

That first night in Hong Kong, Duncan and I really enjoyed our dinner of roast beef, crisp potatoes, and fresh salad. I was not sure what Chris and our parents ate, because I was too busy with my own meal. For dessert we had an English-style custard with raisins.

The next day was planned for lessons so we could catch up a little from so many short stops, and so much history, religion, and culture! Spelling? Arithmetic? Huh?

March 8 - The Peak Tram

AFTER A MORNING OF ARITHMETIC LESSONS and being not too happy to be back in the "grind," as Chris called it, I was excited for our first daytrip of exploring Hong Kong. We were going out to the actual island of Hong Kong.

Getting to the island took about one-and-a-quarter hours if you were lucky! First, we had to take the hotel shuttle bus to the Kowloon waterfront near the ferry dock and then take the ferry across Kowloon Bay to Hong Kong Island.

Chris bought us tickets, and I poked my head up close to the attendant's window where his small abacus lay on the counter. He used the stacks of beads to calculate what we owed, and the change, too. Then, to clear the abacus for another calculation or for the next customer, he ran his forefinger nail across the top and bottom rows, separating the "5" bead and the four single beads. It clicked almost like an adding machine and actually was a kind of adding machine. But it was so different and so simple.

Mostly very rich people lived on Hong Kong Island. The ferry was quiet and had nice varnish work and upholstery. Nobody on board was delivering fish and vegetables! All that happened in small launches and sampans.

Once we got to the island, we started walking and trying to follow the signs. Luckily, there was a picture of a tram car on some of the signs for us to follow, but then we stopped seeing them. Eventually, after losing our way so many times and walking in circles like those "crazy Americans" that we actually were, we finally got to the Peak Tram. It was like a combination cable car and tractor. The island was all hills and rocks. Before the first tram was built, the only way for residents to get home was in a sedan chair carried by two men walking up a narrow path.

Hong Kong – Kowloon ferry lands

The tram made five stops, including one that had only been added a few years ago. The tram track was really, really steep, almost like a sloping elevator and was pulled up and down with chains and gears.

And, it was surprisingly fast. I did not like heights, so I looked up and out to the harbor in the distance, and to either side, but not down!

We got out at the top and we walked around the peak area, which was mostly beautiful homes nestled among trees and landscaping. Servants and gardeners were moving quietly about in their canvas shoes. Except for them, nobody was around. Maybe there were armed guards hiding out of sight?

Once we got back down to the base station of the tram, Chris flagged down a taxi, and the driver took us around the island shore-line. We stopped for a few minutes at Aberdeen harbor, where near-ly everyone lives on a boat or houseboat. Some were simple small boats, some were converted Chinese junks, and some were lavish yachts, but all were rafted up together.

After that, we made our way back to the ferry dock, took the ferry to Kowloon, and then a taxi to the hotel. There was a lot of traffic. Again. It was always busy here, even in the middle of the night when I sometimes woke up. Night was when there was less traffic, so lots of work was being done then on roads and buildings and ships, Arthur told us.

March 10 - Silk, Wool, Dumplings

We did lessons in the morning, after a breakfast of fried eggs and bacon with toast and marmalade. And tea, of course. After some work, we had mid-morning tea in the hotel lobby complete with sugar cubes and little frosted cakes. After that, we went down the mountain on the shuttle bus to downtown Kowloon for shopping and lunch.

We had our first Chao Tse of the whole trip since leaving home, our favorite meat-and-vegetable-filled dumplings. These were a special "number one" favorite for Duncan and me. We had a fami-ly friend who once set a record of eating 126 at one sitting. Once I started eating them, I had to finish the plate. They usually came on platters or in a box of six, but thankfully and hopefully, there were more in the kitchen, or on the cart in the street!

Anyway, they were steamed, or sometimes fried, and then we dipped them in a salty and sweet soy sauce mixture with flakes of garlic and scallion in it. The meat and juices inside the pastry skin, which was best if you could see through it after it was cooked, kind of exploded in your mouth on the first bite. The best skins were rolled by hand to make them extra thin.

Earlier in the trip when we were in London, Chris had made a side trip to his family's homeland in Ireland. While there, he had bought some Irish or Scottish wool cloth to be made into a sport coat. There were custom tailor shops everywhere in Kowloon, making clothing for travelers and businesspeople from all over the world. Chris was going to have a jacket cut and made just for him. He was excited to have something like that because it could last a lifetime.

Hong Kong back-street markets

In Bangkok, Mary had purchased some beautiful raw silk to be made into a suit. This tailoring involved several trips for measuring, cutting, and then basting the cloth together for fitting before it was fully sewn. The basting stitches were long and loose stitches, maybe two inches, in white thread, so it was visible. It reminded me of a wooden boat that was framed but not yet planked. On today's trip, Mary saw the basted suit for the first time. She was a little sad, because the grain of the cloth had been cut going across, rather than vertical, which was what she had hoped for.

There would be additional trips for fitting and final touches like buttons and hem length. Each tailor's shop was different and had its own specialties. I was told that fancy English gentlemen could send their measurements to Hong Kong and have their shirts custom made.

Mary did not care much about clothes and shopping in general, unlike Arthur who was always well dressed. She was well dressed, too, because Arthur bought her really nice things that she liked. But it was not important or enjoyable for her to go shopping. Arthur says he is looking for a watchband for himself in different stores.

Some tailors specialized in making the clothing very quickly. For a price they could do it in three days! Basting was finished on the second day, I was told, for the overall fitting. Then everything sewn together, and the final fitting happened while the customer waited. Or maybe went and had tea and special sweet cakes. Or one of many kinds of dumplings. That kind of waiting is not boring at all.

Anyway, everything here moves quickly, with no wasted motions.

Tomorrow or the next day our parents will be visiting students, scholars, and dignitaries, and doing research in different libraries and government offices. There is something called Yale-in-China where they will also be visiting students and other teachers.

March 17 - A Day on a Junk

OUR PARENTS' FRIEND, Mr. Holmes Welch from Salem, Massachusetts, had been living in Hong Kong and was also a China scholar. He invited us all to go sailing with him and some other people on his Chinese junk. We took a picnic lunch of roast beef sandwiches, cheese, and tomato sandwiches, and hard-boiled eggs, from the hotel. The shuttle bus and then a taxi took us to the harbor where Mr. Welch kept his junk, and he took us aboard from the dock.

Junks drift along under sails and oars

The boat was all-natural wood, only a little weathered, and the cabins were the full width of the boat. There were two masts with no stays, and cotton sails with full-width wood battens in pockets. Mr. Welch told us that this basic ship design, in many sizes and uses, was nearly 1,000 years old.

On the outside, the boat looked very traditional, authentic, and un-Westernized. That was a new word for me in Hong Kong. There was even a wood and bamboo walking rail along both sides outside the cabins and hull, and Duncan and I liked scampering around on this. Inside, the boat had all the modern and Western features you could think of, like a head, berths for two with sheets and pillows, and an icebox.

Alongside was another junk owned by Americans. It had big, Chrysler-car style windows, and masts with no sails visible anywhere. They just had two big outboard motors. It had stainless-steel railings and a big striped canopy over the cockpit. We looked in through the big windows. Down below, there was a stainless-steel stove with an oven.

The other family on our boat included the father, Mr. Isham, and his two boys, aged six and ten. They played cards with us while we waited to leave the dock, and they beat us at War and Go Fish. I could not figure out how that happened.

After we motored offshore for a little while, Mr. Welch anchored the junk for lunch in a small cove on a nearby island facing away from Hong Kong. We went swimming from a beautiful white sandy beach with clear water so bright it made my eyes blink and squint.

The other boys were both nice, but Chris, the younger one, just could not keep still and seemed really nervous.

When we got back to the boat, we were supposed to stop at a neolithic site on the way to the dock, a place called Big Wave Bay, that Mr. Welch had pointed out on his chart. I always liked to see the oldest sites around. But the other boys needed to get back to Hong Kong Island with their father, so we headed back to the dock. We went back to the hotel in taxis and the shuttle bus again. It was a fun day, even with no wind!

March 19 – So Close to China

YESTERDAY, OUR PARENTS HIRED A CAR and driver to take us farther into the New Territories, where we went as close to the Chinese border as was allowed. Americans were not welcome in China, although there were trucks moving back and forth across the border bringing supplies and food. China liked to be able to do business with Hong Kong, and Hong Kong needed many things that were available from China, like water, meat, fresh vegetables, and paper.

There were tall fences with many layers of barbed wire, and lots of soldiers on both sides, but mostly on the Chinese side. The soldiers were standing in groups watching the border. There were raised guardhouses up and down the border in both directions. The soldiers' faces had no expressions at all, and their uniforms were not the dress-up clothing of the Cambodian guards or the Queen's footmen in London. Theirs was just for everyday hard and dangerous work, in plain green pants, jackets, and metal helmets. Mary said their biggest job was to keep Chinese people from escaping to Hong Kong.

Otherwise, there was not really much to see, but our parents wanted to go as close as possible, to see into the mainland of China, where they had lived for many years during the 1940s. They had been in China when Japan invaded, and so they lived for more than two years in a Japanese prison camp until the war ended. Mary said how much she wanted to go back to China someday, and she had that shiny, far-away look in her eyes. Arthur was quiet, too, and watched Mary. I thought he was feeling the same way.

March 20 – Museum Treasures

WE DID CALVERT LESSONS IN THE MORNING, and Chris asked us to write a theme. I wrote one about the trip to Hong Kong Island, the ticket man with the abacus, and the tram itself. It was fun to write down all the details. Our parents did more research at the libraries and at offices at the University in Kowloon.

Pretty often when we were doing lessons, and probably at night after he went back to his own room, Chris wrote home to his family. As I have mentioned before, he wrote a postcard to his mother and father almost every day, with his fountain pen in teeny tiny script. He had told us that he gets 300 words on the postcard. That way his family got a picture and a letter for half the cost of an airletter or aerogramme. I hoped that his mother would keep those. I was really curious about what he said to them about Duncan and me. I think he writes to his brothers and his sister, too.

We had lunch at the hotel with some kind of beef soup that was very good, with bread they made right at the hotel. Then, more arithmetic lessons, and finally it was time for a nap. Doing school assignments is hard work, even though we were just sitting still. Maybe sitting still was some of the hard part! It was a quieter kind of day, and anyway it was raining off and on. The view of the harbor was always interesting, though.

In the late afternoon, our parents arrived back at the hotel with a beautiful model of a Chinese junk; I guess they had been working and shopping! The model was hand carved and had sails and an anchor! They were going to have it sent home for us. It was totally realistic down to every detail.

They also bought us a small abacus and a larger wooden one with 20 rows of beautiful wooden beads. Each one came with instructions in English and Chinese. Both of these, along with the junk model, would be part of our museum at home!

It was getting toward dinner time, so they made some drinks, and then they mentioned visiting a woman named Charlotte Horsmann, an art dealer or broker. She was arranging to have some traditional Chinese furniture made by Hong Kong artisans and shipped back to our family's house. They were very excited about this because it would all be made by hand in the same way it had been for centuries.

We looked at the pictures and they explained where they planned to put the furniture. But first it had to be made, boxed up in wooden crates with lots of padding, and then put on a ship to New York by way of the Panama Canal. From New York it would go to New Haven on a freight train.

Chris had already picked up his sport jacket from the tailor, and it looked really nice. Our parents also had Mary's gray silk suit and Arthur's new watchband with them. I really liked Hong Kong, because of all the kinds of food and artisan things, the smells, as well as the boat and harbor activities. "Never a dull moment," as Arthur often said.

Taiwan

March 22 - Smoke and Gloom

Downtown Taipei

AFTER OUR TWO-WEEK VISIT, we left Hong Kong on a brand-new Japan Airlines Convair 770 jetliner. The DC-3s seemed like years ago.

The Japanese crew members were very welcoming and constantly offered us steamed white cloths and extra tea to drink. It was only about an hour's flight to Taipei at 600 miles per hour. Even a short flight still meant hours of getting to the airport, going through the passport and customs gates, and then all that all over again when we got to the next stop.

Duncan tends bar while Jonny looks after the peanuts!

It was dark and gloomy with rain starting when we landed in Taipei. Outside on the runway when we went down the stairs, it smelled like coal smoke, trucks, and factories. There was no feeling of fresh air coming in off the sea like we had in Hong Kong.

When we arrived at the hotel in our taxis, which was the usual way, the hotel entrance was marked on both sides by bright red glossy pillars holding up painted green-and-blue beams meant to look like a temple, but it didn't at all. We checked into our rooms, took showers, and rested. From the balcony, I looked out at the city through the light rain and smoky air.

Then it was time for dinner at the hotel, which started with wonton soup, already one of my favorites from Hong Kong. The long flaps of the wontons sort of swam in the broth like big flat fish with the green vegetable leaves and ribbons of onion chasing after them. And there were those little thin slices of pork about the size of a quarter that were really good.

Mary had shrimp with snow peas. She liked shrimp because she grew up in the south and they had lots of shrimp caught in the Gulf of Mexico. And also, it was not chicken. Chris and Arthur had a different sizzling chicken dish with green peppers and onions that came on an iron griddle.

Duncan and I had one of our favorites, chicken with cashews, which had little white and green chunks of crunchy vegetables in it, too. And of course, lots of steamy, fluffy rice, and don't forget the soy sauce. The juice in the serving dish, with a little soy sauce added, could almost have been a whole other meal.

At dinner, our parents were talking about "pirated" books, which was something done in Taiwan. Books were reprinted cheaply and without permission, so our parents were talking about books they and others wrote and that were being reprinted in that way. I guess it was a pretty big business here. They were glad the books were available for Chinese students to read and had been translated into Chinese, but still it bothered them, I guess, because actually, it was stealing.

It was still raining and cold. We were all tired and went up to our rooms right after dinner. Mary had offered to read to us, but I fell asleep right away.

March 23 - Real Chinese Food

We took a walk in the morning after a "Western" breakfast of scrambled eggs, toast, and apple juice, and then did some lessons. When we went out, we saw some of the parks and government buildings with Chris. It had stopped raining but was still gloomy. Our parents were working in the archives.

Later, after our parents had cocktails in the living room part of their bedroom, we all went to Zhen (Gin) Beiping (the Real Beiping) Restaurant for dinner. I was not sure how our parents found out about it, because it sure was tucked away and hard to find. Our parents' Chinese language was coming back to them, and it was turning out to be very handy.

The restaurant was right next to the railyard and was shaped like a really narrow diner, up unmarked and rickety wooden steps. The kitchen was in full view, up some more steps and actually hung out over the railroad tracks.

Incoming coal-burning train engines puffed smoke into the restaurant as they came into the yard because the windows were open to get air in and out of the kitchen. Each time the train whistle blew, one of the chefs rushed to close some windows but usually it was too late.

The restaurant was really crowded and noisy, and all the Chinese men were drinking whisky and beer, talking loudly, and smoking cigarettes while they ate. Chopsticks in one hand and a cigarette in the other, and talking really fast, while gesturing with both hands. There were swirling curls and clouds of smoke everywhere, from the kitchen, the train engines, and the smokers.

The dumplings were like nothing we had ever had before. The skins were so thin and the filling had just the right amount of chopped vegetables mixed into the pork. The little flecks of cabbage and green onions along with ginger and garlic, were easily visible through the paper-thin skins.

Arthur said that they were made in the traditional way, where all the ingredients were chopped very fine with a sharp knife, and the pastry was rolled out by hand. The meat was not ground but chopped so it had texture. Grinding the meat actually tore at it and made it gooey, he told us. But chopping was a lot of extra work, and the cooks would have been preparing food since very early morning.

The waiters, wrapped in food-stained white aprons, kept bringing platters of dumplings, with 10 or 12 on each platter. They also brought out steamed vegetables which included cabbage, snow peas, and onions in a salty-sweet brown sauce and lots of small cups of steaming white rice. I had written about it before, but it was still true: just the rice with soy sauce and leftover dumpling dipping sauce with food bits in it was delicious

While we finished dinner Arthur was chuckling to himself. He said the name of the restaurant reminded him of being in San

Francisco many years before, I think when he was in college. There had been a Joe's Restaurant near the harbor practically since the founding of the city, but maybe it had been sold or something had happened. A new restaurant opened up close by called Original Joe's Restaurant. So, he asked, which was the "real original?"

We planned to go back again to the Real Beiping Restaurant as many times as possible. It was loud and smoky and delicious!

March 29 to April 2 - Sun Moon Lake

On the water at Sun Moon Lake

Lots of lessons these last few days, which was okay since the weather had been cold and damp.

We took a first-class train from Taipei to Taijung, Taiwan's second largest city of almost 200,000 people, which was located about half-way from Taipei to Tainan in the south of the island.

Mary was going to do research in the archives in Taijung from documents brought out from China when General Chiang Kai Shek was driven out and resettled in Taiwan. She had explained to us that the Generalissimo, as he was called, was what was left of the Chinese government before Mao and Communism and that he was not from Taiwan. The native Taiwanese people were not at all happy being ruled by the Chinese but had no choice. His wife, also part of the government, was called the Missimo and everyone was scared of her.

On the train there were very posh seats covered in green velvet, and the stewardesses brought us tea, steaming hot towels, and reading materials, including magazines in English. It took three hours, and part-way there the train stopped so they could hitch up to a coal-burning steam engine for the rest of the trip. When we went through the mountain tunnels, black smoke poured into the carriage, and it smelled like rotten eggs.

Once we got to Taijung, we went on with Arthur and Chris to Sun Moon Lake near Puli by hired car and driver for a vacation or what our parents called a "change of scene." Meanwhile, Mary went to do her work in the archives.

Along the lake there were two hostels, and we stayed at the Evergreen Hostel. It was right by the lake and had rowboats we could use. Duncan and I took a rowboat out alone on the lake since it was very calm, and we know how to row small boats. We took turns with one of us rowing and the other sitting in the stern keeping a lookout and trying not to be too bossy. Rowing is fun because it is done looking backwards but going forwards.

On the second afternoon, we took a motorboat trip from the dock all the way around the lake. The mountains were forested right down to the edge of the water, and it was very beautiful because the clouds hung down over the mountains like soft curtains or pillows.

Sun Moon Lake is in the foothills of Taiwan's tallest mountains, and there were waterfalls cascading down into the lake from two sides. The monsoon season would be coming soon, so the air was very humid. Even so, since there was no smoke, the air felt clear and fresh, unlike Taipei, and the mountains were beautiful and refreshing to look at. I guess that was what they meant by a "change of scene."

After two days Mary joined us at the lake so she could have a break, too. Maybe working in the archives and thinking about her history writing without us to worry about had been another kind of break for her.

We liked being at the hostel. It was a hotel, really, but not fancy at all. They had very hot water for the bathtubs, and we could soak for a long time when we wanted to. So relaxing! The rooms looked out over the lake facing south toward the sunshine, and we could see the sunsets though the clouds over the lower mountains to the right.

The food was simple but fresh and delicious, with lots of tea, rice, and vegetables. There were no dumplings, but there were rolls in a thin rice wrapper with vegetables inside that were very good and crunchy when fried. At dinner everyone wore clothes from their days of walking in the woods and sightseeing. Not even the waiters were wearing white shirts and ties. They had blue shirts and long pants with name tags in Chinese and English.

At Sun Moon Lake Chris was on vacation, too, and went off for some walks by himself, and there were no lessons or spelling word lists to teach or drill us on. That, too, was a "change of scene" for him and for us.

April 3 - Mongolian Barbecue

BACK IN TAIPEI AFTER OUR TRIP to Taijung and Sun Moon Lake, we did our lessons the next morning because it was time to send another packet of our homework and tests back to the Calvert School in Baltimore. After that we visited some temples in the afternoon with Chris.

The temples were made with really big timbers of carved wood, and also beautifully polished and painted wood, and metal, too. There was no sign of anyone praying, and no offerings. Nearby there was a Lutheran church and a Methodist church. They were also empty. These were the first churches I had seen since Istanbul.

All the cars and trucks here were made in Japan. Nothing from England, France, or Germany. I asked Arthur, and he filled me in because he wanted to keep me informed and up to date!

Just before dinner time, Arthur told us we would be going to an outdoor Mongolian barbecue when it got dark, about five or six o'clock. We took a hired car down to a part of the harborfront far away from all the ships, cranes, and smoke, where there was sand and mud along the water. I think it was low tide.

It was very dark, and a cold wind was coming across the water. The men there were dressed in heavy hooded wool robes; they had set up huge pots of boiling water or soup, kettles really, propped up on stones, with wood fires burning underneath. Near each pot was a pile of scrap wood, driftwood, branches, and anything else that would burn.

This was not a restaurant at all. I don't know if we paid for the food, but I think maybe the driver did. It was a meeting place for Mongolian refugees, and they prepared food for each other. We put bits of mutton and pork meat and vegetables into the broth and the men fished them out for us when they were cooked. The broth had a salty, smoky, and woody taste, and there were cups of really spicy dipping sauce, too. I had several helpings along with sips of broth.

Mary had explained that when Japan had invaded northern China in World War II, they took many Mongolians prisoners for labor, like slaves, and killed many more. Some Mongolians were uneasy with the rise of Communism and took refuge in Taiwan. This place with open fires was home for them now. The cold along the river did not bother them since it was not nearly as cold as Mongolia! They were laughing and telling stories and passing around some kind of whisky.

There were just a few torches burning on sticks driven into the sand, but otherwise it was pitch dark except for the cooking fires. I stayed close to my family because the large, hooded men with beards were a little scary to me even though they smiled and were not mean at all. In addition to not liking heights, I was afraid of the dark.

I was told that after we finished cooking, rice noodles would be put in the broth to make a soup to finish the meal. All the small scraps of meat and vegetables that remained in the kettles would be in the noodle soup. Everything was eaten. But we had gone home by that time because it was so cold and dark. I bet the flavor of the noodle dish after all that dipping is really delicious. I noticed everywhere in Asia that nothing was wasted.

Luckily, our driver had waited for us; Arthur had paid for his dinner, too. He had enjoyed the food, even though he was Chinese, not Mongolian.

Japan

April 17 - In a Tokyo Garden

IT WAS SPRINGTIME when we arrived in Tokyo, and soft pink-and-purple-colored tree blossoms were coming out everywhere in the hotel gardens and along some streets and in parks. The fruit trees were cherries, crabapple, and pears, I was told.

We had been there for about two weeks, and I had not done any theme writing at all except for what was assigned by the Calvert School.

We were living at the International House of Japan, which was like a hotel but meant especially for people like us who were going to stay for a longer time. We were going to be there for almost another two months. There were other scholars and teachers living there, too. The Japanese really respected scholars and learning, and our parents were known in Japan, so we were treated kindly and respectfully. The atmosphere was almost hushed except for Duncan and me.

We had studies in the morning and sometimes in the afternoon because our schoolbooks had finally arrived from Paris by freighter. A small truck like a boxed motorcycle with one wheel in the front brought the big trunk from the shipping port at Yokohama. The driver needed help from the hotel workers to bring it in because it was so heavy.

We had to catch up to finish the whole year of school before we went home, and we had not had all our books for almost four months. I liked maps so several times along the way I had tried to make a map in my head of the world and see a ship traveling from France to Japan. I thought I could see it traveling around Africa, but I was not sure if that was right. I asked Chris about the Suez Canal, and he showed me where it was on a map.

At breakfast our parents mentioned that our whole family had come to Japan a long time ago when I was six months old. I remembered them telling me before that we came by freighter on a ship from Seattle named the Talleyrand. We had stayed for a year in Kyoto and had lived in a small house on a quiet side street that had sliding rice paper doors and walls. Duncan went to a small school, and I was looked after at the house by a Japanese woman, my "uba," so I ended up starting to babble in Japanese.

Anyway, after lunch and more lessons we had free time, so Duncan and I went to the garden. The hotel was a low, three-story, modern-feeling building, and one of those stories was a garden level below the lobby and used for dining rooms, which you could get to by a very wide, simple wooden stair made of suspended thick planks for each step. The dining rooms looked out onto a patio that would soon have outside tables under the balcony above, as the weather was getting warmer.

Gardens surrounded the patio and the hotel on this side like part of a huge bowl. Part of the patio was made from small stones raked in a pattern with grooves, which we were not supposed to walk on. I was told it was supposed to feel like a lake and the grooves represented tiny waves.

Up on the hillsides surrounding the patio area there were miniature waterfalls with pools, curly old pine trees, and flowering plants. There were some very old trees that looked like sculpture called bonsai, and these have always been very special to the Japanese people. It was fun to explore up in the back area near the fence. We peeked over it and the city was right outside there, with trucks and cranes and noise. But inside it was quiet and the horns seemed far away. Several times a scholar lost in thought or meditation walked by on the paths, but mostly we had the gardens to ourselves.

When we played hide-and-seek, we didn't actually count and go hide, but just quietly escaped and then hunted for each other. Sometimes I forgot to stay in hiding because I saw something interesting and went to look at it closely. For example, there were tiny toads hiding near the trickling fountains, and I liked to watch them move their heads and eat bugs with their tongues.

Later on it got cloudy and colder, so we went inside and had Japanese tea and read in our room. In the lobby it was always possible to get tea at any time of day, served in handmade cups with no handles. Instead, the cups had small dents squeezed into the clay for your fingers. The Japanese tea had a woody taste and light green color and was relaxing. It was not at all like the tea in India, which was usually served strong with milk and lots of sugar.

Japanese people were different from all the other people we had met and knew. They were quiet, polite, kind, and paid very close attention. They respected and honored children. They even had a special Boys' Day holiday. I knew we were expected to do our best to behave and be respectful, too, but Duncan was better at that than I was. I wondered if that would always be true, even when I got older. Was I always going to feel behind?

April 20 - Sad News from Home

YESTERDAY AT LUNCHTIME someone from the hotel front desk brought a yellow envelope to Arthur. He opened it and looked shocked, and his hands fell into his lap. For a while he said nothing, looking down. Then he said: "Whit. Gone." He put the Western Union telegram on the table, and we all stopped eating and sat still.

We knew who Whit was. He was the president of Yale University, and our parents really looked up to him. He had helped arrange for our family to move from California to Connecticut, even though Duncan and I thought it was a terrible idea. Why would anyone leave California and go "back East," where floods and blizzards were happening all the time? Even hurricanes. We had even sat down in the driveway in Los Altos to try to block the car from leaving. But now, back East was home.

In the dining room, we were quiet through the rest of our lunch of soup, rice, chicken, and vegetables. I guessed Mr. Griswold's death was a big surprise and a shock because he was not old. Arthur was usually very calm and said what needed to be said, even though he could be very funny and loved silly movies like the Marx Brothers. At this time though, he was silent and looked at Mary.

Then I remembered seeing Arthur in his study when we lived in Los Altos, staring across the room holding another telegram. Grandpa Wright, his dad, had just died. He looked that day just like he did yesterday. I was five years old then. Arthur did not have any brothers or sisters, and his mother had died a long time ago. He had two cousins that he saw once in a while.

We did more studies after lunch and, at dinnertime, while our parents had drinks on their small room balcony, Chris took us back to Nicola's Steak and Pizza House where we had been before. The pizza was so good, almost as good as in New Haven, with lots of cheese and a toasty crust all bubbled up. We don't get pizza too often at home because we live away from town, so this was a treat. Japanese really love grilled steak and also love pizza. So do I! And especially because it tasted like home. The restaurant was almost completely full. Japanese men were drinking their whiskies and beer, smoking, and laughing.

There was a big open grill with chefs making steaks and grilled meat under a big metal canopy with a loud fan, and a back area where many different sauces were made. Next to them was the brick oven with its Roman style arch (I could recognize those from a mile away), and the pizzas were cooking inside. Everyone in the kitchen was wearing tall white floppy hats and jackets with two rows of buttons, just like my English coat.

They also made the Japanese salads back there, with radishes, carrots, hard crunchy lettuce, and a sweet-and-sour ginger dressing. It was a little like Russian dressing at home but spicier and more interesting. Duncan liked the radishes a lot, but to me they were just okay.

When we got back to the International House, our parents were not in their room, so Chris read to us, and we went to bed. Maybe they were talking more about Mr. Griswold. I thought they were probably out for a walk, maybe in the garden, which had tiny lights at night. It was misty but not raining, and still warm.

April 23 – A Day at the Ballpark

YESTERDAY, ALL OF US WENT to a Sunday baseball game between the Yomiuri Giants and Hanshin Tigers. The Japanese were nuts about baseball, what they call "Basu Boru," and everybody seemed to be rooting for the Giants. People were standing up and yelling and shaking their heads about referee calls. All very polite, because Japanese people are polite and considerate at all times, even when they are unhappy or they disagree.

The Japanese have their own World Series, which isn't really a world series, just like the World Series at home is not either but just the United States and Canada, I think.

We had snacks that included sweet rice balls and small paper bowls of tempura shrimp and little tempura vegetable sticks with a sweet soy dipping sauce. We don't get Coca Cola very often, but it was a baseball game so "all bets were off," as Arthur would say. The grown-ups had Asahi beer which was very foamy on top and gave them each a white mustache until they licked it off or wiped it on their sleeves.

We had taken the subway to the stadium, which almost everyone did. There were taxis and a few cars around, but people were just pouring out of the subway stairs and escalators as we arrived.

I had never been to a professional baseball game at home, but this stadium was huge, and the seating areas were covered by a roof that had no posts to cut into the view. It was getting hot, too, as the monsoon season was coming very soon, so the shade was nice.

When the Japanese take a liking to something, they really do it right. We went to a golf driving range with Arthur last week, and it was under a roof but open to the outside, and there were three levels of places to practice from. Japanese men on their lunch break were whacking away at the balls really fast, no stopping between, like it was an automatic factory for making golf swings. Some men were trying different clubs, swapping back and forth. A coach was helping an older man to develop or perfect his swing, so he was going much more slowly.

Arthur loves golf, but the rest of us did not play. We left after a little while and stopped for pizza after our subway ride.

April 27 - Alpine National Park, Nikko

LAST WEEK, the president of Yale University died. A day or two later, Arthur told us about the plan for last weekend's trip to the mountains. Duncan and I had been working hard on our studies, trying to catch up. I had been studying American history, which did not really make sense to me, with all the rest of the world's history that was all around us on this trip. But that was the assignment. Maybe this weekend trip was going to be another "change of scene?"

Our Friday afternoon train to Nikko left from Shinjuku Station in time to make the two-hour trip before dinner and darkness. Mary had planned it that way. Japanese trains were always exactly on time, to the minute, or even the second. It was a chilly, gray afternoon. We took a taxi to the station and Mary pointed out the many destroyed buildings.

She told us that it was only 17 years since the end of World War II, with the dropping of the atom bombs at Nagasaki and Hiroshima. Tokyo was still recovering from the American bombing of their city. I remembered the ruined buildings in London from the German bombing that looked a lot like these.

Our parents told me Shinjuku was the busiest train station in the world, with over 250,000 people every day! It sure seemed to me like most of them were right there with us.

We got onto the train and took our seats in the rear section of one of the cars. The front part of the rail car, beyond some glass panels with temple scenes frosted on them and other panels meant to look like wood and rice paper screens (called "shoji"), was a traditional area with woven grass tatami mats on the floor and a smooth surface pathway in the center to move easily through the train.

Arthur had told us that older Japanese people could not sit comfortably on chairs and liked the more relaxing and stable feel of traveling with their legs tucked under them. Japan was a place where older people are treated with great respect. Duncan and I had been practicing this way of sitting, which the monks also used in the monasteries and temples for hours and days at a time, and it was really hard, particularly in a moving train. Arthur said that sitting in a chair would actually be painful for an older Japanese person, the same way tatami sitting for hours at a time would be for us.

Already, the forward cabin riders had slipped off their geta, traditional wooden block sandals, wearing just white tabi, or big-toe socks. Some donned simple black slippers before settling onto the mats. One middle-aged woman had a thermos of tea that she poured for her older companions, maybe her parents. Maybe they were going to visit the home of some ancestors?

The train moved quickly and smoothly out of the station, soon traveling north through the bright green glow of early-season rice shoots in the paddies, while dark clouds blocked our view of the mountains up ahead. There was little or no talking. Everyone sat quietly. I think I slept some.

Our weekend outing and stay near the Alpine National Park in Nikko was a traditional leisure activity in modern Japan, we were told and was enjoyed especially by older Japanese. For us, it was a big change from the rush and noise of Tokyo. We had heard that the Japanese would soon be building ski lodges and resorts in Nikko, but nothing like that was there yet.

Our train arrived under the wide canopy of a simple stone building. We rounded up our luggage and made our way by taxi and a luggage pushcart pushed by a small, really strong man, to the wooden timber guesthouse with its steep roofs for shedding winter snow. On the street the smell of charcoal-roasted chestnuts and sweet potatoes was comforting.

Our parents both spoke some Japanese, so our arrival at the lodge was full of cordial greetings, nodding, and smiling. I was learning that even if I didn't say anything I could still be polite, nod a little, and smile. The Japanese, when greeted this way, smiled and bowed slightly in return. Maybe I would try that at my new school next year.

Inside, the main room of the inn was lined with bunks three-high on two sides, with shelves between the sets of beds for clothing, and low tables in the middle on tatami mats. Dark wood, and the sweet garden-like smells of wood smoke and old damp wool, were everywhere. A stone fireplace to one side blazed to take the chill off. Everyone was wearing thick socks, almost like boots, and bundled up in layers of wool.

The sounds of Japanese people talking was something that sounded a little familiar to me, I guess, from when I was in Japan as a baby. Everyone was polite as I have said before, especially with older people. I was tall and skinny and very pale. But I didn't stick out quite so much when I was wrapped up in blankets.

There were cold toilet rooms with cold-water showers for washing at the back of the building beyond the kitchen. Not just icy water, but no heat at all, either. There were separate times for men and then women to use the big steaming wooden tubs that held eight or ten people. That water was really hot, for relaxing, but not for washing. I went in very slowly, about one inch at a time, with Duncan and Arthur.

After our dinner of grilled meat and pickled vegetables with rice, which everyone at the inn shared together at long tables, almost everyone went to bed early in our built-in shelf-beds. Some guests stayed up by the fire, sipping sake, which was very strong Japanese rice wine, and talking softly in the firelight. The crackling fire, the low voices, and the cozy cubby space of my bed put me to sleep right away.

April 28 - In Shorts in the Snow

THE MORNING DAWNED GRAY AND COOL with cloud mist swirling down from the mountains of the national park and through the valley. After a breakfast of a cold egg square with fish and vegetables in it, a bowl of soup with bean curd, and a cup of green tea in our snug, wooden-log lodge, we prepared for our hike in the national park. For the day, my brother and I each had shorts, knee socks, brown crepe-soled oxford shoes, a cotton shirt, and blue V-neck sweaters. We carried our dress blazers, too, just in case.

The day was gloomy and crisp as we set out for the mountain trail in the park, predicted to be a two- or three-hour walk and led by a much better-clothed guide. Duncan, Chris, and I joined the small group of Japanese adult men. Our parents had made other plans for the day.

As we walked up the trail through the tall pines, we soon entered a cloud layer and were wrapped in fog. A little later and higher up, as the trees got smaller and thinner, we came out onto some rock outcroppings with low bushes hanging onto the cracks. There were no trees at all.

As the wind got gusty, Duncan and I felt the cold as it dug in deeper and deeper. With no gloves or hats and no long pants, the wet snow that replaced the light rain showers added to the cold. We later heard that snow is not so unusual at this time of year in the mountains. But for us it was the only snowfall of our whole trip!

As the drizzle turned into snow showers, the flakes got really big, and still our guide trudged ahead. The other hikers turned up the collars on their jackets and hunched forward.

We put on our blazers over our V-neck sweaters when the snow got heavier. My knees were bright red and my hands were, too. Chris was getting tired, too, but he did not complain. He was wearing this new Irish wool jacket that was made for him in Hong Kong, and it sure was coming in handy!

We had no drinks or snacks with us, and stopping would not have been possible anyway with no dry place to sit. We trudged on, trying to watch our steps on the rocks, occasionally stumbling, following along the bare ridges and outcrops.

Finally, we started back down into the forest with its quiet tent of tall pines. We walked a long time, but without any views down to the valleys below because of the clouds. My feet were stiff and numb with cold. After a long time, we came out onto the dirt road into town and returned to the lodge. We had been gone for more than six hours!

"How was it, boys?" our parents asked cheerfully from where they were lounging in front of the fire. I glowered back, rolled my eyes at my brother, too cold to do anything but take off the damp clothing, pull on some pajamas and climb into my bunk, shivering.

A little later, steaming hot rice with grilled meats, lots of tea, and a scalding hot bath definitely helped. But I could not keep my eyes open. I crawled into my bunk, pulled up the wool blankets and I didn't remember anything else until morning. By then, the weather had changed, and bright sunshine was streaming in through the inn windows.

April 30 - The Great Buddha

Kamakura Daibutsu

KAMAKURA WAS A VERY FAMOUS TEMPLE SITE near Tokyo's port city of Yokohama. We went by train for a day trip starting at Tokyo Station, which was almost as busy as Shinjuku. On the way there Arthur explained that he and his parents had made this same trip in 1928, when he was 15 years old. He said that tucked away in an album at home, we have a picture of him visiting the temples.

The last part of the train trip after the main station stop was a two-car trolley down the main street almost to the temple grounds. Actually, it was more like a streetcar. From there, we walked into the park, and it was very hot. We got bottled drinks and bought post-cards. At the far end of the street was the ocean, but we did not have time to go there.

Japanese temples usually had beautiful sweeping roofs that came down and then curled up at the corner with amazing carvings under-neath and along the spines of the roof too. Looking at the roof from inside, I saw the raw logs just as the trees were when they had been cut down, without the bark and not straightened by sawing. On top of these was thatched roofing made of twigs and straw. Lots of birds were nesting in there, and that was fine with the Japanese people.

Where the beams met, they seemed to go through each other and come out the other side, and those tips were also carved with lots of detail. Sometimes the beam ends would go out past the edge of the roof, and so they turned gray and became a little rotted from being outside for so many centuries.

Arthur pointed out many of these details, as he knew a lot from his trip many years ago, and also from studying Buddhism.

One of the main attractions in Kamakura was the huge Diabutsu, or the Great Buddha. It was a copper figure of the seated Buddha that weighed almost 100 tons, we were told. It had been outside since it was made more than 700 years ago. The weather had stained and streaked it on the outside, and the metal was tarnished green by the salty air from the nearby ocean.

Once I got up close, it was too big to imagine how it could ever have been made even in smaller pieces. We walked around and saw the other main temples nearby. It was very quiet even though it was crowded and hot. That was probably because the Buddha was watch-ing everyone from 40 feet in the air!

After seeing the temples, we had noodles and tea in the little town and then took the train back to Tokyo.

When we got back to the International House and had dinner downstairs, our parents took us back up to their room. They let us open a box and inside was a model of a traditional Japanese house, all made of different kinds of wood, and fit together like a puzzle. It had real shoji sliding screens, and bamboo storm shutters. Even the tatami sections on the floor fit together like puzzle pieces and were removable. It had an outhouse, too, with "geta" shoes outside as if a person were inside. It was a very special gift, and our parents were very pleased to see us exploring the model.

They said they were going to have it packed up and sent back home for our museum. It would be in the museum along with our Phoenician and Roman pottery from Byblos, the Greek sailboat model, the bullock cart from Puri, the Chinese junk, and all the coins I had saved from each country.

May 3 - The Earth Moves

Yesterday something really scary happened. We were just finishing lunch in the downstairs dining room of the International House and were looking out over the garden and patio. It was warming up even more than the day before, and there were broken clouds and a little sunshine. I was holding my soup spoon and looking at the empty plate, hoping that more food would be coming.

Then the windows started to rattle. Glasses in the rack by the kitchen door started to clink. Then the whole rack moved, and the wall behind it seemed unsteady. Raised voices speaking in Japanese from the front desk and lobby upstairs carried down the stairs. The big windows moved in and out as if they were not quite solid anymore. A light was flashing on the wall near the door to the patio.

Then the whole building started to shake, the way a close thunderclap rattles and crackles before the big boom. Suddenly something shot through under the concrete floor right by our table. It was an earthquake tremor maybe, but a big one that seemed to lift the floor in a shallow wave as it went by right next to us. Then, as quick as a flash of light, it was gone.

I saw it coming, the way I am used to seeing rain squalls and wind coming across the water when we go sailing. But this was so much faster and made a very low rumbling sound just before it came by.

A few moments later there was another earthquake, but it was much smaller. Then it was all over and very, very quiet for a few moments.

The staff had shouted to everyone to leave the building and to go out into the patio right away, which we had started to do, with Mary on her feet first and grabbing Duncan's and my hands. But everything seemed to have slowed down and was in slow motion. It seemed to take us a long time to stand up and walk maybe 20 feet to the sliding door. But it was all over before we even got to the door.

I did not see any cracks in the concrete, looking in through the glass once we got outside. Pretty soon a waiter came to clear the dishes and waved to us to come back inside. He apologized to Mary and Arthur in Japanese for a long time, including little bows and gestures. They told us he was saying that he was very sorry for the quake and for the children being scared. Arthur told us this with that special smile of his that is half sad and half funny. It was typical of the Japanese to apologize for the inconvenience even though it was not at all their fault.

At dinnertime, Arthur told us about the Imperial Hotel that was not too far away, designed by the American architect Frank Lloyd Wright. It was built on a very shallow curved dish of concrete so it could move in case of an earthquake. I wondered if he was a relative of ours, but Arthur did not know. I was thinking maybe, but Arthur was a historian, so no guess work, and things we don't know about could not suddenly become facts. He promised we could go see Mr. Wright's famous hotel, though.

I kept wondering if yesterday's earthquake moved that hotel building even a little bit. Maybe it was too small a quake. I was wondering how they had made something less solid in order to make it stronger.

We used to get small earthquakes when we lived in California. They would rattle our farmhouse in Los Altos and the windows would shake and the floor would feel just a little soft, but only for a minute. Once, right after I got home from kindergarten, I was changing my shorts upstairs and the earthquake came and shook my pants off.

Then that was it, except for my heart pounding, like waking up from a bad dream. Even when I was only four or five years old this happened to me.

May 5 through 7 - Kyoto and Nara

Hall of Dreams temple, Nara

IT WAS A LONG TRAIN RIDE TO KYOTO on a very quiet electric train, with all Western-style seating. No tatami mats here like the ones in the Nikko train. On the right side of the train, we passed by the famous volcano of Mount Fuji, which they called Fujiyama out of respect.

After we arrived in Kyoto, we visited some huge and amazing temples. One of them had a completely gold roof. There were pink, purple, and white flowers everywhere, with the falling flower petals floating on the ponds and drifting slowly in the wind. We walked for a long time and visited many shops in the old town, which had narrow streets and alleys that stretched up the steep hills.

In the palace for the shogun (emperor) that we visited, no one could sneak up on the emperor while he was sleeping because they had built-in "nightingale floors." The wood floors squeaked on purpose, to sound a warning. We were told there was no possible way for a human to step from the entry or any window and get to the sleeping room without making the floors squeak. The beds where the women slept had porcelain pillows so their hairdos would not get messed up.

That evening, we had a sukiyaki dinner cooked at the table in a really small restaurant where we sat on floor cushions called zabuton. We sat on the tatami around a beautiful wooden table with a gas fire in the middle of it. The very thin-sliced beef was cooked in a sweet and salty beef-and-soy-sauce broth right at the table, along with all the vegetables.

Each person took pieces of food out of the simmering broth with their own chopsticks, dipped the food in beaten raw egg, and then let it dribble for a moment on steaming rice before eating. It was so good. The egg somehow made the food slightly sweeter. When we were done, the waiter put noodles into the broth to make the final soup. This was a little like eating with the Mongolians in Taipei, except indoors, warm, with lights, and sitting down. The sweet and tangy smells stayed on my clothes and were still there in the morning.

That evening after dinner, we stayed in a small traditional guesthouse near the river in the older part of Kyoto. We went to bed early and got up to travel to Nara. Just as we got up, I saw some tall birds wading slowly in the shallow river outside the room, just like they did in traditional paintings.

Nara was a holy site for Japanese Buddhism and was about 45 minutes away from Kyoto by train. It was important because it represented for Japanese people a dignified though simpler time than the present was, which they revered even if they were not Buddhists.

I felt tired and a little bored until I saw the big bronze gong at the center of Nara, outside the main temple with another really huge Diabutsu in it. The hammer for the gong was a log about eight feet long and hung from a timber frame on ropes. To ring the gong, which was not allowed, a person would have pulled the log back and then let it go like a slingshot or battering ram. This would have called the monks or faithful students and visitors to prayer. I bet you could have heard it for miles.

There was another smaller building called the Temple of Dreams, but I did not find out too much about it. We walked around the outside and bought some postcards. Arthur seemed lost in his own thoughts when we visited these ancient sites in Asia. He was calm, though, and happy to tell stories when we asked. Mary was always ready for another longer walk. Nothing could stop her. Every day was like a visit to the Roman Forum or to the Acropolis. Then she would ask, "What's next?"

We took the train back to Kyoto in time for an early night, but not without a tempura dinner of fried shrimp, fish, and vegetables first.

We left on the train the next morning in time to get to Tokyo by the middle of the afternoon. We had been traveling a lot, and this had been our last side trip before we packed up to go home. Our parents told us we were going to have lunch with Mr. Muramatsu in the Imperial Gardens, though, before we left.

May 10 - Lunch in the Imperial Gardens

WE WERE INVITED TO HAVE A FAREWELL LUNCH at one of the private guest pavilions on the Imperial palace grounds by Professor Yuji Muramatsu, a China scholar and friend of Arthurs. He was large and jovial, enjoyed whisky and sake, and deferred to our parents. As I had been noticing during these months in Japan, Japanese people really respected children and treated them very well. The same was true of their feelings toward scholars and teachers. Our parents had always included us in events like this even though I was very young.

Arthur told me that the average adult height of a Japanese person had increased by six inches since the war. So, older Japanese people were often smaller than I was, and I am only 11. I was five-feet-one-inch tall and 92 pounds at my last doctor's appointment according to Mary. My face had some pimples, and I did not like them at all.

The serving ladies at the garden buildings wore beautiful white kimonos with brocaded landscape scenes on them, and wide white "obi" sashes around the waist. They walked in traditional Japanese wooden shoes (only worn outside) called geta. They have two large wooden blocks built into the sole which raises the person up about two inches and tips the shoe forward with each step. We saw older people wearing them in Nikko and on the train, too.

The ladies were sneaking looks at me, with my short blond hair, skinny legs, crepe sole shoes, blue socks, and khaki shorts. I felt like a strange pet without a leash and no place to hide because I was too big. I was studied from behind hand-covered mouths, smiled and giggled at from behind sliding shoji. It was not mean, but I was very shy.

The building was a seven tatami (three feet by six feet traditional-sized woven mat) room, according to Mary. There was another building almost exactly like it on the other side of the garden.

Traditional home interior, Imperial Gardens, Tokyo

Mary all smiles in her drip-dry dress with her boys, Kyoto

Long ago, it had been the city home for a rich family, with two rooms, a place to wash outside one door, and the outhouse to the back. The bedding for all four family members was rolled up and tied with brocade strips each morning and put under a low bench. The bedding was unrolled each night. Everything was still there out of respect, so we could see just the way the house had been 150 years earlier. In modern times, the rooms were used for private meetings and special meals only. We were told that visits were very difficult to arrange.

On the wall was a gold-threaded silk tapestry about six feet by five feet, which was actually a Zen Buddhist priest's robe, according to Arthur. Priests were expected to live in poverty, literally dressed in rags, and so, Arthur told us, this lavish brocade had been cut up into squares and re-sewn back together in a slightly shifted pattern. That way, it was imperfect. But to me it was almost more beautiful in the way it was put back together.

For lunch we had a hot salty soup with bean curd and bright green vegetables, a sweet pickle salad, some cold grilled shrimp, and an egg cake with tiny bits of fish and small pieces of red pepper in it. I drank lots of tea.

We sat on the floor and Professor Muramatsu told stories and jokes with our parents while the grown-ups enjoyed their whisky and sake. Once Duncan and I had finished lunch, we stood up, nodded to Professor Muramatsu, and left to scout around the outside of the houses. There was a garden between that building and the other one that was part of the same residence.

There were natural stones set in the raked gravel, and also a carved stone lantern with a roof like the buildings, and three curved legs. It came up to the height of my chin! These and other garden features were carefully arranged to look so natural and wild, but the plantings were perfectly trimmed and cared for. This is how Japan was for me: nothing messy, everything arranged and organized, but also very natural looking.

Guilford, Connecticut

June 2 – Home!

OUR LAST TWO DAYS IN JAPAN were really busy packing up all our books and all the last-minute things that needed to be done. Most of the books were being left behind for schools in Japan, I think Mary had said. So not that many had to be shipped home.

Soon, Duncan and I would be sanding and painting our boats. But wood craftsmen in Japan didn't use sandpaper at all because it scratched the wood. Instead, they scraped everything with sharp blades, as if they were shaving a beard.

That last night we went to have a special tempura dinner. We had eaten it before in Kyoto, but here it was prepared in a very delicate way. The outside layer was thicker, but not at all soggy, and not toasted brown. It was just barely cooked and smooth but still crunchy. We also had yakitori chicken, because Duncan and I don't like shrimp and fish that much. But the tempura vegetables were delicious, especially the sweet potato and the tiny broccoli heads.

In the morning I could see that everything was in bloom in the International House garden with pink, white, red, and even orange flowering bushes and trees. Some of the flower petals had blown off and drifted down onto the raked gravel area, where they floated like a special arrangement on a quiet lake. Two months ago when we first arrived, the first buds were barely showing, and cold, damp rain was still falling on many days. Now it was warm and humid, and the monsoon rains were coming any day.

After lots of bowing, smiling, and handshaking with the staff at the International House, we packed into two Toyotas for the airport and our trip home. We flew on a Japan Airlines DC-8, the fourth

American-made four-engine jet model we had flown on this trip, along with the Boeing 707, the Convair 770, and the Convair 880. We flew to Honolulu, Hawaii, to get more fuel, and it was a very comfortable flight. As usual, Japan Airlines provided delicious food, lots of towels, soft music, and soft smiles! Dinner was Japanese food, and breakfast in the morning, three hours later, was American-style, as we got closer to home.

Once we arrived in Hawaii, we had to go through customs and immigration. Arthur told us to be prepared for it to take some time. Silly me, I thought there would be lots of shouts of "Welcome home!" and things like that, but the officials opened every pocket of every suitcase, and they wanted to look in our pants pockets before finally letting us through after almost an hour. Then came the welcome with Hawaiian music and fresh Hawaiian pineapple chunks on toothpicks. Mary was given a necklace of flowers called a lei.

Once we arrived in San Francisco, we said goodbye to Chris at the airport, because he was going home to see his family in Boston. Suddenly, the trip was over! It was just the four of us again. No more "Up and at 'em, Jonny boy" from Chris, and I knew right away how much I would miss him.

I remembered that this airport in San Francisco was the same one where I would sometimes go with Arthur on Sunday mornings, riding in his red Jeepster convertible in the years before we moved to Connecticut. We would pick up the *New York Times* after it was flown in overnight from back east.

Chris had taught us for a whole school year, read to us, and went everywhere with us. He cheered us up and calmed me down, which was not always easy. All this writing I had done was because he had us write a theme so often. He had said he thought he would be able to get a job writing for *The Boston Globe*. That would be a good job for him. And he wouldn't have to fit everything on a postcard!

Our parents rented a car, and we went to see their friends in Palo Alto and Los Altos where we used to live, and also their friends in Berkeley. Boris and Difa Hamins, and their son Anthony, were really happy to see us! Our old house in Los Altos was still there, but all the walnut trees and most of the apricot trees were gone. We had just left four years earlier, but the bulldozers had been busy.

Our final flight was on a United Airlines DC-8 to Idyllwild Airport in New York. It was a bumpy ride for the last hour of the six-hour flight. The pilot said there were storms offshore. It was the worst landing of the whole trip. As the plane touched down first on one wheel, it swerved to the left, and then to the right and almost everyone gasped or yelled. The plane finally settled down straight on the runway.

We were picked up by the travel agent who had dropped us off nine months before. We stopped and had a ham and cheese sandwich at the rest area off the Connecticut Turnpike in Milford, then continued home for another hour.

It was after eleven o'clock at night when I slid into my own bed at home. Eight o'clock California time. I lay there, slowly moving my arms and legs back and forth on the smooth sheets like we did lying down in fresh snow and quietly moaned to myself. "Home."

Afterword

IT HAS BEEN MORE THAN 60 YEARS since that final United Airlines touchdown at New York's Idlewild International Airport. We arrived in a fierce crosswind on wet pavement that made for the most frightening of nearly 30 landings during the previous nine months. We were glad to be home and were also perched on the threshold of a new era, as young boys, as a family, as a country, and as citizens of a larger world.

The trip itself was the adventure of a lifetime. I still wonder what drove our parents to set up this complex and metamorphic tour for their boys and themselves. What curiosity, thirst, and vibrancy of spirit launched the idea for the trip? And how did they manage to corral a uniquely well-suited young man to teach and herd those boys through their studies and adventures? As it turns out, they were building their family story out of the mosaics and timber, bricks and columns, archeological remains, and the many mysterious and magical tales we were exposed to during those nine months.

I also know they were searching for archival materials that would spark and support their next research steps as teachers and historians. More than that, they were both in their early 40s and had boys who would soon become adolescents and need a consistent education and circle of friends. Timing was almost everything. Given their earlier travels before and after World War II, they surely wanted to see what had become of the places they had seen and loved.

In all likelihood, they desperately wanted to find a way to get back to China, and they certainly made inquiries at any and all embassies in various capitols, as well as with the Chinese cultural attachés in Hong Kong, Taipei, and Tokyo. How could they get back the great forbidden world of modern China, whose birth pangs they had witnessed first-hand and written about? Only Arthur lived long enough to return to China, later in life.

Ours was a real-time journey that can never be replicated, as the world has become more hostile, crowded, and wary of colonial white people on many continents. India was teaming in 1963, with 450 million living there. In 2024 it surpassed 1.47 billion people. Everything has changed. Kaiser and Hudson cars are long gone, replaced by millions of Indian-made Tatas, and other world brands. To the north and east of India, Mao was in charge of China, but the Cultural Revolution that would ravage and transform the world's largest nation was still years away.

Those nine months shaped and textured nearly everything in my life. Art, architecture, building, design, color, weather, geography, food, language, religion, writing, photography, justice, and all aspects of family life are all themes that surface in this book. Of these, a few have taken up residence on the raft of restlessness that has been my adult life. Writing, building, making, design, food, architecture, color, texture, and justice are all central to my outlook, choices, values, and everyday life.

Chris Lydon has ever so kindly commented that I was an energetic and observant boy, somewhat prone to spates of temper tantrum and indignation. I was young and trying to keep up with a fast-moving experience and four very smart people, all the while curious, and also, curiously, lonely. Even in my journals I would write sentences like "There's just way too much to write about on this day's outing, so I just won't write anything at all." Now, these decades later, I can recover those memories and write them down in detail.

Harnessing creative energy is my best suit, and it guides me in friendship, writing, arts, design, and public life. I see things in a large systemic way, as one would have to, having gulped down the dusty Indian subcontinent in 25 days! When I see children and adults suffering and living in want, the stark contrasts apparent to my 10- and 11-year-old-self return in full color. I feel compelled to make things better.

My life as a parent has been immeasurably enriched by having traveled. My children used to call me the "oracle," before Wikipedia and Jeeves and Siri knew everything, because I retained global-scale information at the ready. I can usually picture a detailed map and the people living there, pretty much anywhere.

As each of our own children reached the threshold of adolescence, Meg or I took them on a special several-week overseas adventure of their choosing: one to Korea, one to Japan, and one to Greece. My Jewish friends often make an Israel pilgrimage during this same developmental age for different but similar reasons. Take your children and grandchildren to unfamiliar places. It does not have to be that far from home!

These stories might have languished in a drawer, or been relegated to a casual memoir, but for the enthusiasm and encouragement of my wife Meg, and the support and guidance of my friend, mentor, artist, gardener, author, and publisher Russell Powell. Then, once I went in, and in deep, the stories themselves pushed up more and more details and recovered memories. As a process, this is a remarkable form of liberation. So, it is true that we can know much much more than we think about in the moment, and our capacities for understanding, empathy, analysis, and changing of perspective, are truly vast and always beckoning. For this I am almost, but not quite, speechless with gratitude.

Acknowledgments

First and foremost, I am so grateful to my parents, my brother Duncan, and miracle-worker-as-tutor Chris Lydon for all they gave me and our family life during this unique time. Chris's writing mentorship for those nine months started a train rolling that, to this day, has no terminus. Whether the real-time train was headed to Norfolk, Chartres, or Kamakura, we were all in this together on and off the tracks!

Duncan has shared the bunk beds and jump seats not only on this trip but for all our early years. He continues to be a steadying and delightful guide in all things.

This book would not have heaved itself into view and onto these pages without the persistent and sparkling enthusiasm, encouragement, and love that Meg Kelsey Wright has given me in my adult life. She read the manuscript many times, editing, supporting, celebrating, and contributing. More than anyone, Meg has championed the uniqueness of this story.

Russell Steven Powell, as publisher of Brook Hollow Press, and a wonderful friend, editor, colleague, mentor, and reader, has been the engine that would not quit. Bar Lois Weeks found the time, energy, and focus to proof the manuscript, reading and commenting multiple times with a keen eye and ear, without which it would surely have unforgivable errors. Thank you, Bar! Over many months my friends at Paradise Copies in Northampton, including Carol, Christie, Tom and many others, laboriously scanned and organized digital images, copied draft manuscripts, and made it all seem easier than it was. Thank you!!

The book design has the fingerprints of Chris Weeks's creativity and attention to detail all over it, to wonderful and enduring effect. Chris's feel for the book aesthetically and as a technical document is amazing, for which I am so grateful. Thank you, Chris, for once again partnering with me and Brook Hollow Press!

Robin Barber was an invaluable reader. He, along with Carol Edelstein and the Wednesday Night writers, have been an inspiration for more than 20 years. Thank you, each and all for your support, companionship, and writing fellowship!

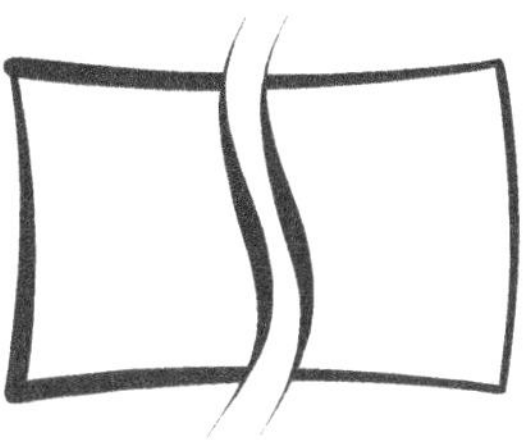

Brook Hollow Press

is a small, independent publisher of print, visual,
and electronic media located in Holyoke, Massachusetts.
Send queries to info@brookhollowpress.net

Also from Brook Hollow Press:

America's Apple (2012)
Russell Steven Powell

A Kentish Lad (2016)
Simon Walsh

Feeling the Heat: Temperature and Time Sensitive (2016)
Russell Steven Powell

Living Without Lawn: Rethinking the front lawn (2016)
Russell Steven Powell

My Interview with James Baldwin (2016)
Russell Steven Powell

Season of Dreams: Two Weeks Alone in the Peaked Hill Dunes (2018)
Jonathan A. Wright

Secrets of a Crazy Artist (2019)
Al Lachman

Rufus: A Boy's Extraordinary Experiences in the Civil War (2018)
Phoebe Sheldon

Molly's 17 Rules for Living: Words to Live By from a Canine Bodhisattva (2020)
Russell Steven Powell

Have You Seen the Ghost of John? (2021)
Christine Copeland

Monkeyface: A Memoir (2024)
Judith Podell